# C.R.I.M.E.

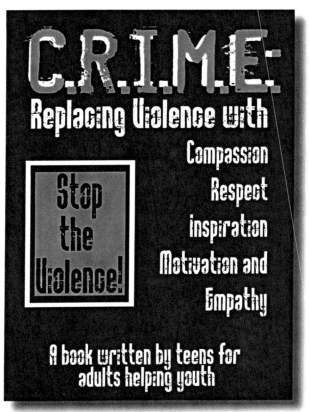

# C.R.I.M.E.
## Replacing Violence with
### Compassion
### Respect
### Inspiration
### Motivation and
### Empathy

Stop the Violence!

A book written by teens for adults helping youth

AUTHORS:
Brandon Copeland, Tiara Ousley, Domonique Ratcliff,
Monique Ratcliff, King Sami, Aaron Shannon, Daria Siler,
and Desiree Tellis

EDITORS:
Jeffrey J. Bulanda, Rachel Kibblesmith, King Sami,
and Desiree Tellis

Books by
BLACK FREIGHTER
PRODUCTIONS

www.welovereading.com

*C.R.I.M.E: Replacing Violence with
Compassion, Respect, Inspiration, Motivation and Empathy*

Is Published by:

Black Freighter Productions
www.welovereading.com

Printed in the United States of America on acid-free paper.
14  13  12  11  10          5  4  3  2  1

Library of Congress Control Number:  2010902391
ISBN 13:  (PBK.) 978-0-9801114-9-1


Text, Layout, and Cover Design: Solomohn N. Ennis, BFP.

Funding for this material was provided through the Illinois Violence Prevention
Authority. The views and statements expressed here do not necessarily reflect
the views and opinions of IVPA.

# DEDICATION

The C.R.I.M.E. Team

Jeffrey Bulanda: I would like to dedicate this book, first and foremost, to all the teens that have contributed to a more socially just, peaceful, and inspiring world through their participation in the Stand Up! Help Out! and C.R.I.M.E. programs; to Dr. Tyson for the example she has set as teacher and mentor, which taught me how to be a mentor to my interns and apprentices; and, to my parents, who have always supported my capacity for "C.R.I.M.E."

Brandon Copeland: I dedicate this book to everyone affected by violence—no matter what age you are. There is still too much conflict going on throughout our communities.

Rachel Kibblesmith: I would like to dedicate this book to a myriad of human connections. First, to my adult mentors who have assisted me in cultivating my compassion and respect: my parents, Dr. Jeffrey Bulanda, Dr. Tyson, Deanna Guthrie, Angela Paranjape, Dr. Julia Pryce, Douglas Wyman, and Mary Heidkamp. I would also like to thank those individuals who have instilled motivation and inspiration in me: our C.R.I.M.E. teens who worked just as hard as we did to complete this project, my clients who allowed me to work with them for their success, and my professors in the M.S.W. program who imparted their wisdom and experience to me. I want to thank those who have allowed me to experience empathy: my siblings, my dear friends and their families, the Murawski family, and any child who I have worked with who has presented their story to me. Finally, I would like to thank those who took a chance on me and allowed me to develop my passion and dedication to the field of social work: Doolittle School, Donoghue Charter School, Forest Road Elementary School, and Project C.R.I.M.E.

Tiara Ousley: I dedicate this book to everyone who has taken part in making it happen. I also dedicate this to those that are afraid and struggling to change. I hope that if they are thinking of change, that they take their first steps by reading this book to cleanse their mentalities, hearts, and spirits. I would like to acknowledge my mom because without her I wouldn't be here, and most importantly Jehovah, because he loves us and all of us wouldn't be alive if it weren't for him.

Domonique Ratcliff: I dedicate this to my godmother who has always told me right from wrong, and to never give up on anything. Also, to my friends for helping me become a better person and not giving up.

Monique Ratcliff: My dedication goes out to my grandma who never gives up on me. I also dedicate the book to all of my brothers, my sister, and my church famliy at West Point Missionary Baptist Church.

King Sami: I would like to dedicate this book to the next generation of teens; know that you're not alone. Also, to my nephews Chin, Will, & Sheed; my brother, Brian, who has taught me many things by being a great role model; and, to my father and mother who continue to mold me into the future man I will become. Finally, I'd like to thank everyone that helped this book become a true representation of C.R.I.M.E.: All my partners of C.R.I.M.E.

(Monique, Domonique, Daria, Desi, Aarron, Brandon, & Tiara) and most of all, Jeff for recruiting me.

Daria Siler: I want to dedicate this book to my sister and niece, Barbra Siler and Sareana Siler-Brown. I also want to thank Jeff Bulanda, Angel Pringle, Rachel Kibblesmith, and all my co-authors.

Aaron Shannon: I would like to dedicate this book to my parents, grandparents, siblings, and my entire family.

Desiree Tellis: I would like to dedicate this book to my mother, Ruby Baker; my father, Deshawn Baker; my sisters, N'kem, Briana, and Delilah; my grandmother, Ruby Wright; my grandfather, Jackie Brown; my Bible study conductor and her husband, Shanta and Ruben Evans; and, the countless other friends who have helped me to become the well-rounded person that I am today and who have instructed me in the overall correct way to live my life and who have helped me to continue to move forward in life.

# CONTENTS

Contents

# FOREWORD

KATHERINE TYSON MCCREA, PH.D.

I'm writing this from my heart to say thank you to the youth who have participated in our Stand Up! Help Out! programs and also especially to the youth of C.R.I.M.E.: Thank you for teaching us! I have been a Professor now for two decades and a clinical social worker helping children and youth for even longer. Of all my teaching and scholarly learning, this book is the best! What these youth have to say to us are pearls that can fortify our hearts and souls.

Remember that the youth authors of this book have grown up under stressful circumstances and face more challenges as teenagers than many people have in their entire lives. Yet the youth have united together and given generously of their time and thoughts to you, the readers. What they have to say is based on personal experiences and also on their careful listening to other children and youth who are struggling with how to handle the stresses of life so as to feel more fulfilled and connected with others, rather than alienated.

The youth of the C.R.I.M.E. project have been so generous and dedicated because they really believe that we can make our society better, and all of our lives more fulfilling, if we focus on Compassion, Respect, Inspiration,

Motivation, and Empathy. And there are a lot of professors, researchers and scholars, who agree with them! There are so many we can't name them all here. Dr. Bulanda names some below and others you might consider include the Dalai Lama, the writings and speeches of Dr. Martin Luther King, Jr., Fr. Henri Nouwen's reflections (1982), the positive psychology movement (positivepsychology.com), Corey Keyes' and Jonathan Haidt's book, *Flourishing* (2003), and the scholars who have been developing concepts of compassion, ranging from the philosopher Martha Nussbaum (2001) to the psychologist Paul Gilbert (2005).

It is fascinating, isn't it, that the youth of C.R.I.M.E. have never read those scholarly works, but they all agree with scholars' and religious leaders' fundamental concepts of compassion? They can describe their own experiences of compassion, and they show us that we have within us the ability to resolve some of our most troublesome social problems: violence, alienation, and despair. Since we all have compassion inside of us, the youth of C.R.I.M.E. tell us that what is key is allowing our compassion to run our choices, free from resentments, fears, and cynicism. For this, they say, linking arms together in solidarity can make a real difference. We need to unite together, inspire and uplift and support each other, so we can live out the compassion we all feel and need. The youth of C.R.I.M.E. are all living testimony to the strength and power that can be unleashed when youth work together and allow their creativity and inner love to be expressed.

Thanks to you, the reader, for your time and consideration in reading this. We hope you will find the youths' messages uplifting, and that their wisdom may come to your aid during times of trial. It is said that during every time of trial, guidance and love will also be present to help the troubled person through. We hope you find this supporting and inspiring as you face your trials and carry out your goals for your own lives. We hope this book helps you remember that reaching out to connect with compassionate people, as these youth have, will help you to thrive.

Katherine Tyson McCrea, Ph.D.
Professor
Loyola University of Chicago School of Social Work

# ACKNOWLEDGMENTS

## THE C.R.I.M.E. TEAM

This book was created in the context of multiple partnerships with individuals and organizations that are committed to creating a socially just and peaceful society.

First and foremost, we want to thank the Illinois Violence Prevention Authority for believing in the mission of C.R.I.M.E. and providing the funding to make our vision a reality. We appreciate the technical assistance and support offered by Sara Moffitt throughout our project. Further, we thank the Youth Advisory Board for allowing the C.R.I.M.E. group to continue fighting violence through 2010 by renewing our funding. We also want to thank all of the schools and agencies that allowed us to present the ABC'S of Peace during this school year.

Next, we would like to thank all of the support from Loyola University Chicago. Dr. Katherine Tyson McCrea has offered her undying support and commitment to our programs since the beginning; we appreciate her efforts in managing many of the administrative aspects of this grant as well as her invaluable consultation in running the program. We want to thank Dr. Jack Wall, Dean of the School of Social Work, for his ongoing support in expanding the Empowering Counseling Program and his willingness to use university resources to make a true impact with our programs. Certainly, one of the most valued aspects of our projects is the incorporation of media into our presentations. Without Dr. Elizabeth Coffman, Professor at the Loyola School of Communication, this would not be possible. So, we want to thank her for facilitating the ongoing collaboration between the Schools. Thank you to Doris Allen for making sure we always had a place to meet and the materials we needed. Finally, we want to thank everyone at Loyola who has assisted with the grant administration: Dr. Bill Sellers, Cora Dahon, and Tom Vloedman.

The idea of C.R.I.M.E. evolved from our *Stand Up! Help Out!* After School Matters program. Therefore, we would like to thank After School Matters, in particular Trinanein Almo and Tony Diaz, for supporting our program since Summer 2006. We thank Mr. Todd Barnett and the staff at Donoghue School for giving our program a home and giving our teens an opportunity to develop.

We would like to acknowledge all of the individuals in the Bronzeville community that have been our partners since the beginning. Bernard Clark has worked with us closely in promoting violence prevention and is truly an inspiration in the community. Principal Lennix of Doolittle Elementary School is committed to giving her students as many opportunities as possible to transcend the violence in the community. Finally, Andrea Lee is an amazing community organizer committed to educational equality for students in the Bronzeville neighborhood.

We want to thank our editorial board of adult helpers that worked closely with us in putting together this book. In particular, thank you Scarlett Stoppa, Carrie Colpitts, and Jim Joyce. We appreciate you giving up so many of your Saturdays to help get this book together. Of course, this book would not be possible without our publisher, Solomohn Ennis. Thank you for teaching us about the "biz," seeing our unique talents and putting them to use. We would also like to acknowledge Patty Hart, a regular guest speaker to our programs and a last minute editor; we appreciate your thoroughness in proofreading our book and your passion for helping teens.

Next, we would like to make a special acknowledgement for Angel Pringle and the apprentices of *Stand Up! Help Out!* Angel exemplifies the mission of C.R.I.M.E. and is an inspiration to anyone that crosses her path. She is loved and respected immensely by everyone in C.R.I.M.E. Finally, we want to thank the other teens in *Stand Up! Help Out!* You are inspirations as you serve as amazing mentors for the youth at Donoghue and we thank you for your contributions to this book.

Finally, we would like to acknowledge the entire C.R.I.M.E. team: Jeff, Rachel, Monique, Domonique, Tiara, Brandon, Desiree, King, Daria, and Aaron. Everyone has volunteered so much time to try to impact violence in some way. We will always remember our time together: our writing workshops in Room 853, our favorite pizza D'Agostino's, the talks with the younger kids, and our times just getting to know each other while in the car, on the bus, or eating. We have set up a legacy that we hope more teens will follow.

NO CIRCLE IS MORE VICIOUS THAN THE ONE SET UP
BY THE FALLACIOUS ASSUMPTION THAT WE ARE UNABLE
TO CONTROL AN ESSENTIALLY VIOLENT NATURE. ASIDE
FROM THE RESPECT IN WHICH IT PROVES ITSELF TRUE,
THEN, THIS BELIEF IS NOT ONLY INACCURATE—BUT ALSO
DEADLY. WHILE THE VARIOUS OTHER PSYCHOLOGICAL AND
SOCIAL FACTORS THAT CONTRIBUTE TO AGGRESSIVE
BEHAVIOR CANNOT SIMPLY BE WISHED AWAY, ASSUMPTIONS
ABOUT THE NATURE OF OUR SPECIES CAN BE—AND GIVEN
THE STAKES, MUST BE—RECONSIDERED.

—KOHN

# INTRODUCTION: YOUTH AS CONSULTANTS IN THE FIGHT AGAINST VIOLENCE

JEFFREY J. BULANDA, PH.D.

Tuesday, December 1, 2009, this was the day violence became more real than ever for me. Over the past ten years, I have heard hundreds, probably thousands, of tales of violence—school fights, child abuse, domestic abuse, bullying, rape, and so on—while working as a social worker for at risk youth. I have listened to kids; I have consoled kids; I have cried with kids. But, this experience was different.

My after school program for teens located in the Bronzeville community in Chicago—ironically, a program committed to social justice and bringing about peace—let out at 7PM. The teens left and I stayed behind to talk individually to a couple of teens. At 7:05PM, commotion entered the school. Two teens with tears in their eyes and piercing screams yelled, "They're jumping on Rena! They're jumping on Rena! Come out, Jeff!" I walked into a scene of mass chaos. At least thirty-five teens and adults were in the middle of the street, swearing, threatening, and fighting each other. The anger in the air was overwhelming and suffocating. My eyes immediately searched for Rena, the target of the violence. When I found her in the sea of bodies, I tried to shepherd her back into the school, but a police officer scooped her up first. Then, I noticed Nicole, **a straight-A, honors student**, was the one person on the scene bleeding. As is so typical, it was the innocent bystander, who was injured the most seriously. I quickly ensured that she made it back into the school; meanwhile, the police broke up the melee and all the participants scurried away.

So, what caused this violence? If you listen to the kids' talk about the triggers, they will tell you it was gossip on Facebook. Yes, Rena and a former friend gossiped about one another on Facebook. Her former friend then arranged for her associates and family members to show up at the school when Rena was being dismissed from the program. A group of six girls jumped out of their car as Rena walked to the bus stop. Almost immediately, neighborhood teens and adults entered the chaos. It was then that they began hitting any one in their way and Nicole soon fell victim. But clearly the causes are much more complicated than that. The youth live in a community where crime has risen at least 35% in the past 5 years; in a neighborhood where people tend to live below the poverty line, job opportunities are scarce, and even basics such as health and mental health care, good grocery stores, safe streets, food and clothing can be very hard to come by. Parents may be caught up in cycles of violence themselves and be unable to set positive role models for their youth and help their youth find ways to resolve their conflicts without violence. Indeed, some even cause their children to feel that violence is the only way to salvage one's dignity. Deprivation and gross inequality engender deep resentments and anger as we all know, but where can the anger be expressed? Sometimes all it takes is a small trigger and the anger at so much more comes out, and unfortunately often at people who are similarly hurt.

4 |

A lot of what we do in our youth programs is help the youth have a perspective on what their anger and hurt is really about; to unite together to find common and effective solutions to the problems that cause the anger; and to help each young person have reasonable and realizable hope with which to counter the anger and despair.

To the credit of all the youth involved in the conflict, no one was seriously injured, the fight did stop quickly, and has not recurred. It is also notable that the youth came and found me to help as soon as it started. This says to me that it is important and very meaningful for all the youth that we were there! It is also interesting to note that our C.R.I.M.E. group and our After School Matters group were able to have profound discussions about what had happened and how to prevent anything like it in the future. During those discussions, the youth shared that events like that conflict were commonplace, and so we realized even more the need for the activities like ours that emphasize the value of alternatives to violence.

While fights like those I experienced on December 1, are frequent in most any inner city school, this was a surreal experience for me. I just remember walking into a cloud of anger and displaced pain. It was after this event that I experienced "Secondary Traumatic Stress" for the first time. This is when a helping professional experiences traumatic symptoms after being exposed to the trauma of their clients whether *in vivo* or through narratives of his/her client/student. This is a condition that I have lectured about to my social work interns in working with traumatized youth, but it was always more of a theoretical phenomenon than a reality. However, for the week after the incident, I struggled with insomnia, vivid nightmares, and some anxiety about returning to the scene. Certainly, this was a *fork in the road* in terms of where my career would go.

This experience might have dissuaded some from entering dangerous inner city environments in an effort to prevent violence and help youth develop. It prompted me to question what I had been doing and whether my work of the past four years had positively impacted this community. This incident seemed to crush everything we had been working for. However, my C.R.I.M.E. teens quickly put this experience in perspective. You see, the most valuable lesson I have learned in working with these teens is that for every **one** teen on the South Side of Chicago that may plan a mob "jumping," there are **many, many more** teens like the ones in our C.R.I.M.E. program that are committed to preventing violence and becoming mentors and role models to younger children. So, after this affirmation, my passion to join the effort for violence prevention only intensified.

After having my own internal conflicts about the utility of violence prevention efforts, I soon became angry at the irresponsibility of the media. It is a shame that it is the violent teens that are recognized by the media, and that, therefore, the public perception is quite the opposite of my realization. You ask the average person who has never entered and met the residents of communities, such as Bronzeville, and they will likely think that for every **one** resilient, positive teen, there are **many, many more** violent, antisocial teens—quite the opposite of reality. It is my hope that this book begins to break that stereotype.

This chapter will provide a background of our involvement with the Bronzeville community, explain how C.R.I.M.E. came into being and its contributions to the violence prevention effort, and outline the organization of the book.

## BACKGROUND OF THE PROGRAM

C.R.I.M.E. is a part of the Empowering Counseling Center (ECC), a larger effort to serve the youth and families

6 |

of the Bronzeville community initiated by the School of Social Work at Loyola University. In 2005, Professor Katherine Tyson McCrea, with the support of Dean Jack Wall, joined a partnership with the Chicago Housing Authority, local schools, local social service agencies, and other Schools in Loyola University Chicago (School of Communication, Law School, and Business School). The need for social services in the community was profound as the Madden-Wells Housing Projects were being torn down and replaced by mixed-income housing. A number of families were being displaced and violence had been escalating.

As the partnership formed, I joined the effort in 2006, serving as Program Director. We have three primary programs currently within the ECC: the clinical internship program, the *Stand Up! Help Out!* After School Matters program, and the C.R.I.M.E. violence prevention program.

Upon entering the community, we realized that there were few options for child and adolescent therapy services, so providing such services became a priority. Many schools and agencies in the area were seeking social workers to provide services, but did not have the resources to hire social workers or have clinical supervisors for interns. We then instituted an innovative internship model, whereby adjunct faculty at Loyola would supervise interns, who are placed in under-resourced schools and agencies. Since Fall 2006, 20 interns have provided social work services to a number of schools and agencies on the South Side of Chicago, including Doolittle Elementary School, Woodlawn High School, Woodson Junior High School, NKO Elementary School, Price Elementary School, Heartland Alliance, and Abraham Lincoln Centre.

We discovered through administering a community needs survey to the residents that finding after school and employment opportunities for youth was a priority. After writing a proposal, we were funded for our first

| 7

After School Matters program in Summer 2006 and have, subsequently, received funding for every proposed program since. After School Matters (www.afterschoolmatters. org) has an apprenticeship model, whereby adult mentors train teen apprentices in their trade and the teens, in turn, receive a stipend. Our program, *Stand Up! Help Out!,* is an apprenticeship in social work, whereby the teens are trained in the principles and practice of social work. Responsibilities for teens in the program include: mentoring and tutoring younger children, taking social action through peace marches and nonviolence forums, hosting community health fairs, and creating documentaries in collaboration with Dr. Elizabeth Coffman and students from the Loyola School of Communication. Documentary topics have included: violence prevention, environmental awareness, awareness of international human rights issues, and domestic violence. See www. StandUpHelpOut.org for more information.

## Background of C.R.I.M.E.

This book is the product of the most recent addition to the Empowering Counseling Center—the C.R.I.M.E. nonviolence project. C.R.I.M.E. is the result of a youth-led mini-grant funded by the Illinois Violence Prevention Authority (www.ivpa.org). To qualify for this award, the program must demonstrate that the youth are leaders in all aspects of the program from the grant-writing to implementation to evaluation.

When I heard about this funding opportunity, I asked several teens in the *Stand Up! Help Out!* program if they wanted to be involved and write the grant. Five teens enthusiastically volunteered their services and the brainstorming commenced. They began with trying to figure out a "name" for the group and they bounced a number of acronyms around until they decided on the word CRIME. They appreciated the irony of a violence prevention group called CRIME and soon filled out the words that would make the acronym: Compassion, Respect, Inspiration, Motivation, Empathy. Without any adult prompting, they saw that to prevent violence, they had to work to develop pro-social skills and values among youth at risk for being violent. From there, they fleshed out their hopes for the project: teach younger kids about bullying, anger management, conflict resolution, and self-esteem; make a DVD about those skills; and write a book for adults.

To date, the C.R.I.M.E. teens have accomplished everything they set out to do. Accomplishments include:

- Created presentations on the ABC'S of Peace and made an accompanying workbook and DVD.
- Presented the ABC'S of Peace to over two hundred school age youth at schools and after school programs in Chicago and surrounding suburbs.
- Assembled this book, which involved over 15 group writing workshops in addition to independent writing assignments.

| 9

## C.R.I.M.E.'S Contribution to Violence Prevention

Certainly, youth violence has been gaining increased attention among researchers and policymakers who have been exploring causes and potential interventions for the problem (Elliot, Hamburg, & Williams, 1998; Farrell & Flannery, 2006; Graczyk & Tolan 2005; Singer et al., 1999; Tolan, 2000; USDHHS, 2001). Theoreticians and researchers have looked at youth violence from a number of perspectives. A small sampling of these perspectives includes:

- A consideration of the developmental pathways of violent youth (Loeber & Stouthamer-Loeber, 1998)
- Risk and protective factors and evidence-based programs (USDHHS, 2001)

- Social-cognitive information processing (SCIP) theory in understanding violence (Crick & Dodge, 1994; Huesmann, 1998)
- An understanding of the broader context of a violent youth though an ecological model (Bronfenbenner, 1997), and
- A competency/Positive Youth Development perspective (Guerra & Bradshaw, 2008).

So, where does our C.R.I.M.E. book fit among the violence prevention literature? Well, this book is primarily written by the youth that witness and/or experience violence on a daily basis; further, if you consider their life stories, they have many of the risk factors identified by the statistics (single-family homes, victims of violence, living in low-income neighborhoods). Despite all of the risk factors, they have found ways to transcend their circumstances. These teens are the *experts* on violence prevention because they have lived it. Certainly, many researchers and theoreticians have provided invaluable insights and research in understanding youth violence, but I want to emphasize that the C.R.I.M.E. teens are also an authority—if not, *the* authority—on this subject. Their authority should not be undermined by their age or lack of post-secondary education, which often occurs in our adultcentric society (Petr, 1992; Zeldin, 2004).

While this book may be written in layman's terms and have a limited bibliography, it is a relevant source on violence prevention. Indeed, one can readily convert the insight and knowledge offered by these teens into the fancy theoretical terms valued in academia. For instance, when Daria Siler writes about how the use of physical punishment is passed on from parent to child, she eloquently describes what family therapists call *intergenerational messaging*. Certainly, Ms. Siler has never read a family therapy book, but she has lived with the consequences of intergenerational messaging and reflects on those personal experiences in her chapter. Such discussions and personal narratives add validity to this book that is missing in purely theoretical models or articles about "evidence-based practices" that treat humans as statistics alone. It is also crucial to have this "lay" perspective on violence as the teens are reaching out to the adults and teens who do not have access to the academic journals, but who need to think about and take action on these issues.

## THE C.R.I.M.E. PERSPECTIVE ON HUMAN NATURE

In September 2008, five teens were left alone in a room in Donoghue Elementary School and asked to come up with a project that will help reduce violence in their community. C.R.I.M.E. was born. What started as a catchy, fun, ironic acronym actually represents a profound shift in understanding why violence occurs, how it can be prevented, and the nature of human beings. Rather than suggesting they teach the kids about the consequences of violence (i.e. Scared Straight) or teach adults how to discipline acting out kids (i.e. behavior modification), the teens decided they wanted to focus on developing the values and skills they felt all kids are capable of: compassion, respect, inspiration, motivation, and empathy. Instead of thinking of the kids in their community as being deviants that need to be squelched and controlled, they saw kids who are violent as missing out on these five core principles of C.R.I.M.E. While they may be missing these values, they saw the younger kids as having the *potential* to live and experience them.

Alfie Kohn (who the teens did not have the opportunity to read) really began this shift in paradigm with his book *The Brighter Side of Human Nature*. Contemplating how we, as humans, tend to think of

| 11

ourselves and our nature, Kohn writes:

> It is evidence of a widespread belief that our darker side is more pervasive, more persistent, and somehow more real than our other facets...We raise our children, manage our companies, and design our governments on the assumption that people are naturally and primarily selfish and will act otherwise only if they are coerced to do so and carefully monitored. (1990, p. 4)

Then, he challenges this belief with:

> There is good evidence to support the proposition that it is as "natural" to help as it is to hurt, that concern for the well-being of others often cannot be reduced to self-interest, that social structures predicated on human selfishness have no claim to inevitability—or even prudence. (p. 4)

Beyond the scope of discussion in this chapter, Kohn goes on to describe the function of this negative view of human nature and then shows scientific evidence that empathy and altruism make up as much, if not significantly more, of our human nature as the selfish, aggressive parts that often get our attention. Such a belief supports my point earlier that for every teen that attacks another, there are tens, if not hundreds, more that are *intrinsically motivated* to join the war on violence—that is, they do it on their own volition and do not need to be bribed or coerced.

What does this shift mean and what are the implications for violence prevention? If adults come into working with youth with the idea that they are capable of compassion, respect, inspiration, motivation, and empathy, interactions will be much more fruitful than seeing them as immature, incomplete, incompetent humans that need to be controlled. Certainly, adults need to provide structure for kids and teens to help them regulate themselves, but adults also need to have an increased awareness of youth competencies and what they can offer. Adults should

12 |

focus their attention to developing these values, rather than focusing on achieving nonreflective compliance from youth. Further, it has been found that adults, who focus on developing teen' self-determination within healthy, satisfying relationships, can actually shift teens' initial extrinsic motivation (motivation dependent on rewards and punishments) into intrinsic motivation (motivation to relatedness, accomplish, and stimulation) (Bulanda, 2008).

Perhaps of greatest importance, by embracing a belief that youth are competent, adults will learn that youth can be effective consultants in how their homes, classrooms, schools, and/or communities are run. So, I hope you read this book with an open mind, seeing these youth as consultants that will help you become a better parent, teacher, social worker, policymaker, researcher, or administrator.

## OVERVIEW OF THE BOOK

| 13

The book is organized as follows:
- Chapter 1: The teens write about C.R.I.M.E. from their perspective and the violence they are attempting to address.
- Chapter 2: Each of our eight teens share a time that violence affected them. They discuss the lessons they learned and bring attention to the frequency of violent actions in their lives and neighborhoods.
- Chapter 3: This chapter presents an analysis of results from when the C.R.I.M.E. teens surveyed 40 other teens living in their community about their experiences with violence.
- Chapter 4: The teens flesh out C.R.I.M.E. For each principle, they give a definition, describe role models that demonstrate the principle, discuss how the principle is seen in "everyday life," and then offer advice to parents, teachers, and the

media in how to develop that principle. It is our hope that each of these sections will serve as a springboard for readers to discuss with the youth they know and encounter.

- Chapter 5: Daria Siler applies the principles of C.R.I.M.E. to a controversial issue that the teens felt strongly about—the use of physical discipline. Ms. Siler argues that using such punishment halts the development of compassion, respect, inspiration, motivation, and empathy in youth.
- Chapter 6: The teens explain the ABC'S of Peace. They describe how they taught kids about anger management, bullying, conflict resolution, and self-esteem with the hopes that readers will use some of this information in working with youth.
- Chapter 7: Teens from the Bronzeville neighborhood offered to write letters to adults about how to stop violence. This chapter features those letters.
- Chapter 8: Each of the eight C.R.I.M.E. teens is interviewed and discusses his/her experience in the program. They also give advice to kids and adults for preventing violence.
- Chapter 9: Rachel Kibblesmith, co-editor and MSW intern with the project, reflects on her experience working with the project and what she learned from the teens.
- Chapter 10: Co-editors Desiree Tellis and King Sami consider "Where do we go from here?" They passionately ask adults not to allow this to be another anti-violence book that "collects dust" and go on to argue how people need to change themselves to impact change on the community level.
- Afterword: I summarize some of the key themes and findings that I discovered in reviewing this

book as well as in watching C.R.I.M.E. evolve into a powerful movement against violence.

We hope you enjoy this book and begin to start seeing your child's development and the problem of violence through the lens of C.R.I.M.E.

# PART
# ONE

# CHAPTER 1:
# PROJECT C.R.I.M.E.: A YOUTH-LED APPROACH TO VIOLENCE PREVENTION

THE C.R.I.M.E. TEENS

## WHAT IS C.R.I.M.E.?

C.R.I.M.E. is an acronym for the words Compassion, Respect, Inspiration, Motivation, and Empathy. With these words we teach children better ways to react to violence. C.R.I.M.E. is a youth led program that creates awareness about violence, actions that lead to violence, and positive ways to avoid them. With C.R.I.M.E., we plan to make communities better places. We as the C.R.I.M.E. group wrote a grant for our program so that we could spread our knowledge and tips to conquer violence and crime. We wanted to advance our organization even further to show adults as well as children that there are teens in society that want to help others become all that they have ever dreamed to be, while making our communities better places. Our hopes are to introduce our program to kids through presentations and to talk to adults about how to help kids avoid violence with this book. Overall, our plan is to continue to whack out crime!

## THE VIOLENCE WE ARE FIGHTING

Violence has been a part of life on this planet

since the beginning of time, from verbal abuse to domestic violence to race riots to civil wars to world wars. The violence that really captures our attention is the violence we see and experience in our own lives. In Chicago, for instance, there has been an unfortunate trend of increases in gang violence and domestic disturbances. According to the *Chicago Tribune,* the city ended 2008 with 510 homicides, up 14.6 percent over 2007 and the most in five years (Rozas, 2009). What is more disturbing is how many of our local youth are killing and being killed. In the 2006-2007 school year, 32 Chicago Public School students were killed. In the 2007-2008 school year, the tally was 26, and in the 2008-2009 school year, the tally was 27 (Rozas & Sadovi, 2008). Sadly, we are on track in the 2009-2010 school year to blow these figures out of the water.

Violence is not just hurting someone physically, but also causing them mental or emotional suffering. Mental violence can be perpetrated in many ways. Teachers, for instance, inflict mental violence on their students when they share their beliefs as if they are facts, when they address behaviors they do not like with sarcasm and insults, and when they ignore students who are in need. Examples of ways that teachers use their face and body to mentally attack students are to turn their back on them, let their face go blank as if they have not heard the student, roll their eyes, sneer, or shake their head. School security guards commit the same kind of violence when they act like they cannot be bothered. This is especially frustrating because security guards are hired to serve and protect the students. Teachers are hired to educate students to be better citizens. These adults need to demonstrate the qualities students should have so they can learn from their examples.

Parents also commit mental violence when they misuse their authority. Some ways that they do this include: putdowns when addressing a problem, frequent negativity, and insistence that they are the boss in all situations. When parents lead in this way, children and teens feel like they do not have a voice. They feel powerless, and then they attempt to get power by using their own forms of violence. Once again, adults need to realize that children have legitimate pains, perspectives, and opinions.

Emotional violence is a particularly harsh weapon when dealing with children and teens as they are still learning how to manage their emotions. Ways that people commit emotional violence include prejudgment (making assumptions about someone before you know them); laughing at someone; gossip; trying to make others look bad; being secretive; insults; harassment, such as relentlessly picking on someone's sensitivities; ignoring people's reactions and needs; snubbing, as in ignoring someone completely; dealing with conflict through passive aggressive actions; thoughtless words; threats; and manipulation. People who carry out emotional violence seem to get some strange satisfaction out of making others sad, mad, or hurt. Perhaps they have their own issues with self-esteem and they feel their own power when they can instigate these reactions. Even in instances of self defense, people who use violence are trying to gain or hold onto their own personal power.

In some situations, mental and emotional violence lead to physical violence. Examples of physical violence include tripping, pushing, kicking, slapping, smacking, scratching, biting, pulling hair, wrestling, punching, strangling, beating with weapons (or objects turned into weapons), cutting, burning, molestation, rape, kidnapping, and shooting. What starts on the playground as small losses of control can quickly escalate to lethal violence in the teenage years and adulthood. It is a shameful fact that we do the most violence to those we know and love. The US Department of Justice estimates "the number of spouses (mostly women) threatened with a deadly weapon is almost 2 million annually." (Buzzle.com) In fact, half of all American households experience domestic violence at least once a year and half of wife-batterers also regularly assault and abuse their children.

It is not enough to know the forms that violence takes. We have to ask ourselves why incidences of violence are trending upward. For teenagers in particular, they sometimes feel like violence is the only way to express their strengths and feelings. Sometimes they feel this way because they have not felt free to voice their opinions. This happens when they have authoritarian adults who tell them that their opinions do not matter. For instance, the police are an ineffective resource when they brush off kids who come to them with information. Teachers who pass "problem kids" on to the discipline office rather than addressing the issues and school policies that send these same kids out to the street with suspensions and expulsions contribute to these effects. Of course, we cannot ignore the issues that come with lack of resources: single-parent households trying to raise several kids, overworked parents, too many students in one class, and so on. Either role models are completely absent, or they are so stressed that they are dysfunctional. This is a perpetual cycle, but it can be broken. And that's where C.R.I.M.E. enters the picture.

# CHAPTER 2: HOW VIOLENCE HAS AFFECTED US

## PERSONAL NARRATIVES FROM THE C.R.I.M.E. TEENS

### THE BUS RIDE
*AARON SHANNON*

It started off as another regular day of school. I woke up, took my shower, got dressed, gathered my things for school, and hopped on public transportation from the Westside to the Northside. This story took place in my 7th grade year at A.N. Pritzker Elementary. I had taken this trip numerous times without any problems. Things changed as I was coming from basketball practice around 7:30PM on the #12 Roosevelt bus.

As I got on the bus everything seemed pretty calm. I walked to the back of the bus, put my music in my ears, and laid my head against the window. I slowly began to fall asleep. About 20 minutes later, out of nowhere, I heard a loud bang right next to my head. My body jolted into an upright position and my eyes were extremely wide. Everyone on the bus was screaming and crying. I had my headphones on and I was sleeping; I didn't really know what was going on. But as I slowly turned to my right, I soon realized someone shot at the bus. The bullet had hit the bus exactly where my temple was lying against the window. All I could do was cry. Someone called 9-1-1 and I called my grandmother to come get me. The medical team examined me and the police asked me questions. I couldn't answer any questions because I was half asleep and still in shock from what had just taken place. I believe it was a work of God that the bullet didn't go through so I would be able to tell my story.

This experience opened my eyes. I realized that life is a precious thing that should be taken very seriously, because it can be taken away at any point in time. This one unfortunate event in life impacted me in a good way. It showed me that people in the world really need positive role models, inspiration, motivation, and empathy in their lives. If that one bullet had come through that window, it would have taken away a big brother to six younger siblings, a nephew, a grandson, and a son. That one bullet had the potential to take away a person that is the role model for six lives. There are many people in the world who have it worse than I do and that alone makes them sometimes do bad things. If they are not cared for, they may not care about others. Or, if they think life "did them wrong," they may not see hope or a reason to try to live a good life. But no matter what takes place in my life or around me, I must continue to stay positive, motivated, and inspired to take my life to new heights.

## A Day at the Beach
*Monique Ratcliff*

One day my friends and I decided to go to the beach. We grabbed our towels and bags and went straight out the door. After a quick walk to the beach, we found our spot. It was sunny outside, birds were chirping, a nice breeze offered relief from the heat, and the smell of barbecue filled the air. All we could think about was getting in the water. It looked pretty and refreshing. Waves gently rolled to the shore. My friends and I dropped our towels and bags and jumped right into the cold water. After the initial shock of cold, the water was a welcome relief from the hot sun. We started to play a game of Marco Polo, splashing around blindly in the water and having fun.

During the game, one of my friends noticed three girls looking at our bags. Before we could get out of the water, one of the girls snatched a bag and ran away. My friend quickly jumped out of the water and ran after the thief. She ran across the sand and finally caught up to the girl and said, "Hey what are you doing? That's not yours, give it back!" Her answer was to hit my friend with some kind of metal piece. My friend's nose looked like a gang of people had all taken a turn punching her. As we approached her, she was lying there unconscious with her nose busted. My first reaction was "wow." I didn't know what to do. My heart was beating as fast as a drum roll. I was in total shock. I could not even move. It was terrifying to see my friend so violently attacked and left unconscious and mauled. I felt bad that I didn't make it there in time and that I was unable to help stop the violence.

While we made sure my friend was okay, the two other girls ran away with the rest of our bags. In the midst of our shock, I thought about how the day affected me. We were just minding our own business. It made me think: I can't even go to the beach for a couple of hours without someone taking my belongings. From the experience I learned to be aware of my surroundings and to never leave my things behind. It also taught me to be the bigger and better person by not resorting to violence even to retaliate.

## THE BEST BIRTHDAY OF MY LIFE
*DARIA SILER*

As a child, I grew up around a lot of domestic violence. Violence can affect children in the most unexpected ways. Most of the men in my family were abusive due to alcohol and drug abuse. These substances cause you to be unaware of the things you do, make unwise decisions, and become a complete stranger to your body. There was never a day when my family got together that there wasn't an argument or a fight, and in the end I was always the one left crying or hurt. I dreamed of having a family like the Cosby's, but I woke up to reality at the age of nine. I knew then that every family has its own issues and it's up to you to either work them out, or just continue to let them go on. I wanted to deal head-on with the issues. The life-altering experience for me came on my Mom's 36th birthday.

My dad had been gone all day with his friends, while my mom and I spent quality time together before night came. We went shopping for an outfit she planned to wear that night to the club. It was so beautiful. However, 9:00 p.m. soon came and there was still no sign of my dad. I was enjoying watching my mom have a good time with her friends. From then on everything passed like the speed of light. In walked my dad, drunker than I had ever seen him. He hadn't been drinking in a while, so it surprised me. I knew my mom was angry.

"Where have you been?!," she questioned.

"Out!" he replied.

The somewhat reasonable conversation soon escalated into an argument and then a fight. I cried hysterically for my dad to stop as I watched him hit my mother, but he was too focused to even hear me. After what seemed like forever, the fight ended and my dad passed out on the couch. He had ruined her birthday. She didn't go out and her friends left, but I knew she was hurt both on the inside and out. The next day my dad awoke to find that my mom was avoiding him and he didn't know why, so he broke into tears. The more I explained to him about what happened, the more he cried. After feeling sorry for what he had done, he apologized to my mom and vowed that he'd never drink again. For at least two months our home wasn't the same, my mom and he rarely shared a room, spoke, or even hugged. My home didn't feel like home at all. When my dad made a nice dinner for all of us and apologized to my mom, she forgave him. Things were still a little rocky afterwards, but we got through it. My dad has been clean ever since, and he doesn't hang around the people he used to because he feels like one day he might have a relapse if he is in their company.

     After the incident, I decided never to get involved with an abusive man that drinks and further, to never drink myself. Seeing the violence between my parents was hard for me as a child. I really didn't know what to do about the situation, but I got through it and I've made good decisions as a young adult. After the huge incident, it took me some time to actually trust people again. I felt that since my dad could betray my trust, anyone could. It was also very hard for me to watch my mom be so weak-willed and it taught me to become a strong independent person because people, even people we love, are capable of doing harmful things to take control, including making a person feel as valuable as dirt.

## Bacteria
*King Sami*

Infection. Yes, my life has been infected by a bacteria—a bacteria called violence. It is hard to find to the words to talk about how violence can infect a person's, especially a child's, life. Sometimes, violence is experienced by a person, then is used involuntarily; the person does not realize where the anger and violent tendencies come from. I want to tell my story to show that one does not have to be violent even if they are taught it and surrounded by it.

Witnessing violence before the age of five years old shaped me into a distrustful individual. We lived on the Far East side of Chicago at 81st and Burnham—a neighborhood where drug dealers and gangbangers run the streets. My two older brothers, each one year apart, were at the living room window talking. I remember this window because it was huge compared to my small size. Suddenly there was a quick knock at the door and a thump. My father opens the door and my oldest brother is there holding his head, with blood running onto his clothes and dripping onto the wooden floor. My mother then runs toward him with a 101 Dalmatians sheet and she covers his face, wiping the blood and trying to slow the bleeding. My brother had just been pistol whipped coming from Church's Chicken on his payday with an $81.00 check.

My second eldest brother gets a 2x4, puts on some boots, and rushes out of the house taking a swing at the wall, leaving debris in the hallway and a mark representing his involuntary use of violence. I see the ambulance come. At my young age, I do not fully remember what was said, but it included killing the assailants. My father stresses to my brothers, sister, and me not to let any one of us go out into the night by themselves and never to split up; we're a family. My mom could not imagine one of us fighting while the rest of us were watching. "One fights, we all fight," she would say.

That was just my first memory of violence; there have been many more since. One evening it snowed about two to three inches and my mother was about to cook; everybody was excited, but to cook you need groceries. I was chosen to run the errand, but I argued my case that I always go and being young I said, "Tell Tony to go because he never does." Neither my brother nor I wanted to go, but we came to an agreement. He went.

It seemed like it took my brother forever to come back from the store. I became anxious and worried because Parkway isn't always as welcoming in the dark as it is when the sun is up. I opened up the door and took a peek out to see if he was coming. My nerves began to bug me. I slipped on some shoes and went down to the entrance of the complex to see if I could spot him. He finally returned with a *bang, bang* at the door. He dropped the bags. There was snow all over his pants. He said that some people had tried to rob him. They attacked him so he had balled up and got kicked and punched while still clinging to the groceries. Instantly, I put on my pants and grabbed a ski mask and two poles that broke from our bunk beds. The objective was to search and destroy whoever attacked him. That's when my mom's boyfriend, Mickey, stepped in and said it wasn't worth it because my brother wasn't hurt. My brother only has one eye and knowing that just sent me over the edge. Violence enveloped me, including itself in my life whether I wanted it to or not.

Mickey stopped that incident of violence, but he certainly was no angel. I never really got along with my mother's boyfriend. My father left us and I continued to grow up and my pride grew as well. After my dad left, my mom introduced my brothers, sisters, and me to the new guy named Mickey. Turns out there's a lot of irony in his nickname. When you think of "Mickey," you think of Mickey Mouse; Disneyland; a beautiful, fun place. Not too long after they started dating, Mickey became violent towards my mom in our home. He was paranoid that my mom was going to reunite with my father. I was taught never to quit, even in doubt or when matched in strength, like David & Goliath, so my reaction to the whole situation was to fight, even kill Mickey for hurting the woman who brought me into the world. At a young age, these thoughts were suffocating in my mind. What made me feel even worse was that every time the abuse happened, my mom told me she could handle it. My father kept saying, "You let him hurt your mom. I would have killed his ass." It was always hard to justify my non-violence in this re-occurring situation. Although the violence has stopped, in some cases when violence is present, you do not have control over whether or not it goes away. This was one of those incidences, but I stayed committed to keeping a cool head. We have control in how we react to violence so that we can refuse to continue the violence.

Violence is like bacteria, it spreads. One way to help prevent violence is to have a mentor or someone you can talk to about the anger and emotions you are experiencing. You can't avoid violence whether it's in T.V shows, video games, your community or your home. However, you can prevent violence by focusing your energy in healthy ways. I prevent violence through my engagement in sports. Don't let the bacteria spread!

## THE ALLEY
### BRANDON COPELAND

It was close to the afternoon. I was with Robert and his friends. Robert's friends were in need of money so they offered Robert and me an opportunity to help them obtain some cash. I replied "no" and Robert did the same.

Around three-to-five minutes later they saw an older man around his 60's. The group said, "OK, wait here across the street," and they entered the alley where the old man was heading to get home. Robert and I became nosey and walked close to the alley. They pulled out a fake gun, which was supposed to be used for an arcade game. The man wasn't shocked at all. At first, he didn't want to listen to them when they told him to put up his hands, but after getting threatened he slightly raised them. The group pulled a wallet out of the man's pocket along with a box of cigarettes. As they opened the wallet, the man had around $100-150. My eyes got wide when I saw that money. After they took what they were looking for, they dropped the wallet on the floor. One of the kids hit the man in the back of his head with his fist, sending the man stumbling. My heart started to pump adrenaline. I felt paranoid. Then Robert and I sprinted out of the alley, taking a shortcut behind a house. Meanwhile, the group jogged to the main street excited about getting new outfits with their new stock of money.

After the incident, I hadn't told anyone except a couple of my friends at school. They weren't too shocked to hear it because it happens around their area all the time and some of them even do it themselves. When that happened, I had to stay away from the area for a while because Robert and I didn't want to get accused.

Later I noticed that behind the store were cameras, but they sure didn't help! So after seeing this, I learned that neighborhoods are never safe—no matter what technology there is. Worst of all, this happened all out in the open where everyone could view! Maybe people weren't paying attention. Or, maybe people didn't care. My hope is that hearing this story makes *YOU* care!

## A Sunny Day Turned Dark
*Desiree Tellis*

I've never really committed violence in my life or have had violence targeted towards me. But I can't lie; I have been a huge witness of it. I must say life is not all peaches and cream, especially on the streets of Chicago. From gang violence to school violence to domestic violence, I've just about seen it all. The things I've seen affect me emotionally. One experience that I can relate has to do with community violence.

I was in the park enjoying a beautiful day. The sun was out, the sky was clear. Everything was just perfect. While I was in the park, I had seen some old friends of mine and decided to converse with them and catch up. We were just talking about how life was going, school, our families, and so forth. It was as if I was in my own little perfect world.

There were a number of families outside barbequing and playing games. It just seemed like a pool of fun, but all fun has to end at some time. The end of this fun was none other than violence. As I continued to talk to my friend, out of the corner of my eye, I just noticed a load of people crowding around. At first, I didn't pay attention because I was so into my conversation. All of a sudden, I heard a scream. Along with the scream, I saw a girl who had gotten pepper sprayed. Her face was red and her eyes were bloodshot. This caused havoc to break out. All I saw were parents looking like they were about to fight. One of the parents even pulled out a knife—a huge knife for cutting cake. However, she couldn't go through with her plan because the police came.

When I sat back and observed this it made me think: What's happening to our culture? Why must there be so much violence? This is just an example of community violence, but I have another experience that is even more shocking. This time it had to do with domestic violence. This experience almost brought me to tears. One day, my mom and I had gone to the gas station. As I was sitting in the car waiting on her to come back, I recall seeing a boy and a girl fighting. This boy smacked his girlfriend up against a car. She tried to fight him back, but she was too weak. With the little strength, she had she continuously tried to fight back, but he was continuously pushing her. My mother saw the same thing, got in the car, and called the police. We never knew what happened after that for we had to leave, but this made me see that even those who love you can harm you.

These observations of violence have helped me to see that the best way to avoid violence is by being careful when it comes to who you hang with, who you trust, and what you do. As I practice these three things, I have been able to avoid violence directly, but that doesn't stop the pain from watching the cycle of violence that surrounds me in my community and school.

## THE JUMPING
### DOMONIQUE RATCLIFF

It was a very sunny day and I was at home. I thought that since it was a nice day that I would go for a walk, so I went outside. As I was walking down the street I saw a group of people. I kept moving and was thinking about what was going to happen. As I was walking, I saw a person headed toward the group. I thought this person was going to say something to them. As soon as I turned my back, he jumped another person.

It really affected me to see someone get jumped on because he got really hurt and the people that did it saw him hurt. I felt sad because looking at someone who got attacked was terrifying and watching him in pain was difficult. When the person got jumped, there were only a couple of people around, eventually, people started coming out of their homes and called the police.

I was thinking, "Should I leave or stay and see what people outside are telling the police?" I felt like I should just go. I felt like there were enough people out there. As I was walking off, I was thinking that I felt really bad about what happened but when the police came that made me feel a little better. I knew the police were going to help with what had happened. What happened that day really affected me and makes me think a lot. I don't think that I should go anywhere by myself and I need to watch my surroundings because anything can happen.

## A Sweet Nightmare
*Tiara Ousley*

Yesterday was a great day, until that something happened. You all are probably wondering who's talking and what I am talking about. Well my name is La'tasha and I'm fifteen years old. I live a pretty good life but I'm really angry right now. I want to get revenge, it should have never happened. I mean, I told him to leave but no, he wanted to act like a kid and stay. I got something for him, it's really good. Yep. I bet you all know what I'm talking about. But first let me tell you how yesterday was.

It was a Friday, my third and last school day of the week. My dumb phone rang and it was 7:30AM Ready for the school day I knew it was time for the usual routine, brush my teeth, wash my face, take a shower and get ready to take the bus. It was just one of those days. I was running late for school, taking my time because, Hello, I'm a girl...it's called hygiene! Anyways, I was in a rush, I grabbed my cell phone and book bag and left for the bus. I got on the bus and arrived at school around 8:30AM I was really excited thinking, "Who would I meet? What will today's lunch be?" Just really excited. But as soon as I stepped into Kaldek High, I felt tired. I went to my first period class early for the first time. But I had to wait till the bell rang. So I sat in a desk in the hallway and cracked jokes about myself just trying to make it easy for me to meet some new people. I shook hands with my peers, which wasn't really me. I knew in that instant that high school would help me better identify myself.

Time zoomed in on me so fast. It was my 8th period lunch and as usual I met up with my good friend Kaliah. I was like, "Hey girlllll I hope lunch is good today," (saying it in my *heyyyy girl* silly way). As we talked I peered around the pretty lunchroom. Unique faces were smiling and having a great time. I felt this good vibe about the school.

Something I haven't felt in a long time. That's when I knew I would begin to love school all over again. But as I looked around, I saw the goof-off boys. I heard them talking about some girl in the room, "She's fat." I'm thinking to myself, "They bogus." Then Kaliah and I started talking about them. "I don't know who they think they is talking about someone when they is ugly as ever," I said. "I know right, he ain't even cute," Kaliah replied.

That one moment pulled my eyes away from the pretty view of the city sitting on the side of us. My mind flew back to that second that I was beat up by a boy in 8th grade. I could hear light footsteps dashing on the ground right behind me and an unexpected wind hit my back. But I kept walking, paying it no attention. Then besides all of that I soon felt agonizing pain. I turned around and fists pounded my face. It was my ugly, skinny, classmate "Lawrence."

I ducked and tried to swing back but saw that I was missing and ran away to toss my book bag on the ground. My little sister was now behind me and trying to fight him back. I gained some courage from the anger and pain that burned inside of me and chased after him. I ran after him but somehow the fear sunk to my legs, and kept me from doing my athletic trick and I couldn't grab him like I wanted to. Somehow the fear sprung and bounced into my fist because I was swinging awkwardly and I couldn't reach his face. I let my height ruin where my fists were supposed to be. My mind automatically realized that it had become screwed up because I forgot about his stomach. He ran away and so I cried and screamed hysterically because I was very angry.

The school's lame security guard ran to me and I was making the ugliest face ever, crying because my pot was past its boiling point. And I saw ugly Lawrence around a crowd of students. I miraculously gained back my athlete trick and jumped on his back and started beating him on his back and wherever else my fists felt like. I let each knuckle get revenge for my bleeding lips and aching head.

My sister should have never argued with him, and then I wouldn't have gotten hit. But I guess it wouldn't have mattered anyway because I heard him and his boys didn't like me so something was bound to happen. He knocked me off him and the security guard was behind me and my mind and eyes raced back at the ugly boys sitting in front of us.

Back to the present time: I looked around thinking to myself, I'm so blessed to be at this school. I really do love school. I don't have to deal with fights and ugly Lawrence like I did at my old school. So I'm done with lunch, we still have time left, and this girl has to take care of some things. Kaliah and I spent the rest of the lunch hour running errands around school, we checked into college information, picked up some planners and then headed to class. During our errands, I joked, "I can't be going to school every day and it being the same. I like something spontaneous." She laughed and started smiling. See, I knew we was going to be good friends, shoot, she was honest with me when I asked her if my I.D. picture was jacked up. The rest of the school day skipped by so fast and soon I was on the train home.

I got home and wasted time doing noon routine because it's Fri-day! My mom came home early. I was like "dang!" because she's annoying sometimes and I asked my sister "Why didn't you tell me she was coming? My sister who already made me feel salty by tricking me into thinking our mom got me some restaurant food told me she had a day off. So I just lay down all day and watched late night shows.

"La'tashaaa!!!" I heard my mom calling and so I walked into the bathroom surprised. She hugged me and

| 39

told me she loved me. It was a beautiful hug, a mother's sweet gift. I heard those words before but she started telling me things I can't recall ever hearing. "La'tasha you know I love you and you mean the world to me?" I nodded my head yes. "You're very special, you and your sister are. You're my first born and you're going to grow up to become very successful and beautiful."

Then it hit me, she has said that to me before it was always either after some stressful moment that would happen or when she drank every now and then. I looked at the bathtub and saw some type of liquor sitting on the edge of it. She always becomes really sweet when she's drinking. "I'm sorry for yelling at you, but you gotta start moving a little faster. You're in high school now." I'm thinking to myself "This is weird." She's saying this like she's about to die. It meant a lot to me. She tickled me and hey I was laughing. You ain't supposed to do that to this girl. I thought I wasn't ticklish anymore. So she gives me a momma kiss and I go back to my room and lay down in my bed. Thinking how years ago I once had a nightmare of her getting killed and how it's just like in the movies. People always saying good things before they die and I fall into my once in a while deep sleep.

Hours later I awoke to hear my sister talking on the phone. I asked her what happened. She told me everything. My mom and her boyfriend got into an argument and he went into the kitchen and got a large, thick, kitchen knife and was about to kill her. Who is he to have the nerve to try to kill my mom when he's always bringing up how he misses his mom and how he wishes she was still alive whenever we complained to him about our mom's bad ways? Then he wants to try to kill my mom? I've been telling him to leave, since he says our mom makes him so mad. He wants to act like a little kid, it's okay because I'm getting revenge.

My sister Aisha told me how she went into the room and yelled at him. Then he stopped only because he didn't want to go to prison. I fell into a deep sleep again, thinking that it would all be over but it turns out I was wrong. I woke up to hear my sister tell me how our mom and her boyfriend had gone downstairs and they were arguing again. Aisha said she snuck downstairs and grabbed the knife off the ground and yelled at him when he choked her up against the car. I could picture it all in my head. My mom's so small compared to him. I was really angry with myself. Why did I have to fall into a deep sleep? I would have come into the room before things escalated. Aisha said he ran away on his bike and our neighbor called the police on him. The police came and arrested somebody selling cigarettes on the streets and just sat in their car laughing at my mom. I was thinking to myself, "These cops ain't nothing but a piece of feces, they are what they let loose. Jehovah's going to take care of him and them." My mom came in and I fell asleep thinking *"My mom could have been killed just like in the movies."* I had my usual nightmare rampage. Nightmare after nightmare struck my mind. I jerked up from my dreams, my heart stabbing my chest, and breathing heavily. My sister made fun of me calling me a drama queen and I fell back asleep. Nightmares, they always follow you, you dream them, you live them, and they chase you. But my nightmare rages ain't gon ever stop me from being the success I'm meant to be.

# CHAPTER 3:
# RESULTS FROM OUR SURVEY:
# WHAT OTHER TEENS HAD TO
# SAY ABOUT VIOLENCE

### Aaron Shannon, Tiara Ousley, & Daria Siler

Violence is something that affects the lives of millions across the world every day. It affects people of all ages, sizes, and walks of life. No matter how perfect a person thinks his or her life is going, they will likely experience violence at least once in their life. Violence, for the most part, is just a way people show emotion or their fears. To learn more about these every day experiences with violence and why they occur, we gave a survey to 40 teenagers on the South Side of Chicago. In this chapter, we review the questions and collective answers.

*Can you talk about a time violence has affected you in your life?*

The first question we looked at was: Can you talk about a time violence has affected you in your life? Based on our results, we came to the conclusion that violence is broken into three different categories that we labeled: domestic, street/gang, and general. Domestic violence is the violence that occurs in a household or violence that affects someone emotionally and mentally at home or with loved ones. Street/gang violence is violence that occurs when people are beaten or killed for no obvious reason, either due to gang shootings, when someone is robbed, or even someone being "jumped on" in the streets. General violence is the violence that happens almost every day, such as fighting inside of school or someone who gets picked on for no reason. In the next paragraphs, we are going to review the results for each of these categories.

Out of 40 people who received the survey, only 4 teens openly admitted to witnessing or being a part of domestic violence (that is still 10%!). We guess that more of the individuals we surveyed have experienced various types of domestic violence. They may have chosen not to answer for different reasons. Some may have never experienced domestic violence; some probably did not want to talk about it and felt like it was none of our business; or, some could have just skipped the question for other personal reasons. But, in any case, we find it a little strange that only 4 of 40 had experienced domestic violence because we know many of our friends and classmates experience it every day.

Domestic violence affects the entire household— not just the person being abused. For example, one of the teens wrote, "Violence has affected me mentally and physically. As a kid watching my mother be a victim of violence, it was a very bad experience." This person witnessed his or her mother experience violence and he or she felt powerless to do anything about it. Another teen had a similar experience, saying "My mom and her boyfriends fighting. I feel paranoid a lot and always think I hear screams and fear my mom's dead." The stress and pain this person had to go through is something he or she will never forget. This is an example of why parents need to think about their kids if they are fighting or arguing with their partner. Sometimes the influences of street crime come into the home, like this person who said, "When I was seven, my brother got arrested right in my face and crashed my party. I felt sad and hurt. I thought it was all my fault." It sounds like this person had their seventh birthday party ruined by having the police take their brother away. Even all these years later, the person still remembers how bad he felt and how he blamed himself.

Street violence is a major issue in many communities that individuals have to deal with on a regular basis. There are so many deaths every year due to street violence. People of all ages are being killed or critically injured because there is unnecessary violence taking place. People should not have to be scared to go outside or go out somewhere to enjoy themselves.

According to our survey, 13 people reported that their lives have been affected by street violence. Out of those 13, three people lost either a friend or a father due to gang violence. For example, one person wrote, "Violence affected me when my father got shot and killed and it really broke me down and I felt sad and depressed." This means a father figure and potential role model has been taken away by something that could have easily been avoided. Because of violence, this person's father is dead. This made the person depressed which probably affected his or her school work and attitude toward others. Because of senseless violence, this person's life will never be the same.

| 45

Other teens were honest about being involved in street violence. For example, one person wrote, "I get into a lot of group fights. My family tells me I should stop or I will get killed in a fight." Being worried about getting killed in a group fight is something that no teenager or his/her family should have to deal with.

The third category we came across is called "general violence." This category consists of random types of violence that pop up in different environments like schools. Violence is a major problem in the public schools in Chicago. There are children who have been killed or seriously injured because of violence. Children are fighting every day and some days end in a real tragedy like Derrion Albert (this case is discussed in greater depth later in our book). Some kids accept fighting as "normal" because of the neighborhood they live in. When asked about how violence affected this person, she or he responded, "You know the regular, gun shots, mob action." This person seems to expect to see violence on a regular basis. This is what we mean by "general violence"—violence that seems to come out of nowhere and for no reason but is consistent. Some examples are: "My sister had got into a fight when I was out of town, when I got back, she had a black eye," "when I was fighting some people at school, it was rough," and "when girls in my home area were fighting."

When the teens responded to the questions, very few talked about their feelings concerning violence. But, three people stated that they were "used to" violence. That is a horrendous feeling to have. No one should live in a neighborhood where violence is second nature. There are different reasons they may be "used to" violence.  It may help them not worry so much about it or they have never experienced something different.  But if people are too "used to" violence happening, no one will take action to prevent it. This may lead to a pattern of chronic violence.

*Why do you think people are violent?*

One flick of the remote and you see on the news how someone got shot, and one step outside and you see someone get stomped or beat. There is not one day that passes by without a child crying because they lost a loved one. Are there solutions to these everyday tragedies? To find that answer, we asked other teens to write about

why they think people are so violent. We received a
lot of different reasons which we put in the following
categories: "it's been taught," they are missing love, anger,
lack of resources, gang affiliation, and survival in this
crime-infested world. Violence has gone so far in our
present day, that it is hard to even find out how it started.
But, we want to look closer at the reasons that the other
teens gave about why people are violent.

## It's Been Taught

When we questioned why people are so violent, we
often received answers that we put into the category "it's
been taught." What is meant by that is that when you have
been raised in a home where domestic violence has been
active, especially when you're young, you become immune
to it and adapt. Some examples of responses are: "Because
it's all they know," "they maybe grow up in the wrong
home," "I think people are violent to show off or prove
that they are bad in some type of way or maybe they were
raised at home around domestic violence and they figure
that's the only way to get [their] message [across]," and
"because others in their family are violent."

Children have family members that end arguments
and disagreements with violence. In turn, a child
unconsciously learns that this is the way to behave and
to solve disputes. When they constantly see this at
home, it is only natural that they would bring this same
behavior outside. When the child acts aggressively, no one
steps in and teaches the child that this is not the way to
act. It just lingers in the child's mind and when nothing
is said, the parent's actions are basically saying it is okay
to behave like this. They are not learning positive problem
solving techniques, so their ways of how to handle certain
situations are limited to violent lessons. All of these are
ways that violence is being taught, creating a negative

impact a child's mind. Eventually this could take a toll in a child's reactions to certain situations and encourage a child to act out violently.

## Missing Love

When a child is not given love at home and is constantly being abused verbally, physically, and emotionally, or is raised around domestic violence, it should not be shocking when he or she adopts violent behavior. When all of this is combined, it is very hard for the child to love and to stop their violent ways. Those missing love have a hard time caring and showing empathy for others. If someone does not care and does not have empathy, it is easier for them to become violent.

## Anger

In this category the teens described how anger thrown out in unhealthy ways is the cause of violence. Some examples are: "Cause they went through a lot. They be angry," "I don't know, maybe because they have problems in their homes and feel like they have to take problems out on others," and "they try to release their anger." Children are born into the world knowing nothing, so the environment around them and their guardians' teachings will either affect their future actions in a negative or positive way. The same goes for not teaching them anything at all, because that can do just as much damage to their behavior. When parents display anger destructively or in an unnecessary, excessive manner, rather than in a calm, proper way, their children will grow to show just as much anger, with just as much OR MORE violence. This unhealthy display of anger leads many children to suicide and/or homicide.

What children learn in school also will affect the ways they cope with anger. Some children are being bullied or may be the bullies, and it is all because someone's angry. They become so angry because of the hardships at home that they may take it out on those at school. They do not know how to control their anger. These children grow into adults that become so stuck in their ways that violence is their only way to go when they are angry. These bottled emotions that children have can be life threatening because they end up putting themselves and others in danger, especially when they become older.

How do we stop anger from turning into violence, shootings, rapes, and so on? It is a lot easier to teach a child the simplest rules about handling anger because they are still growing whereas adults are more fully mentally mature and more resistant to making changes. It is similar to teaching a child a foreign language; they pick it up quickly and they grow to become experts on it. However, when you are grown, it is more challenging because it is harder to pick up. Parents need to start helping their kids learn how to deal with anger from the start of life. Also, teachers do not necessarily need to take some time away from math and spelling to teach students how to deal with anger; they can include discussions and activities about anger within the existing curriculum.

| 49

## LACK OF RESOURCES

In this category, we found such responses as "They don't have anything else to do" and "because of the home and maybe missing parents or poverty." Poverty is everywhere and people are hopeless about how they can get by without having to struggle. Ever since the recession, it is even harder out here in the world to survive. This is another reason why people are so violent because they feel that the only way they can get what they need is by hurting others. It is their way of surviving in this world. We know people in our lives that rob or sell drugs because it is the only way they can provide for their children. Although, there are places where a person can get the resources they need, it is usually not in the distance they can travel or not enough.

It is not just lack of food or clothing that causes people to become violent, it is also not having anything to do. When a person has so much time and they have nothing to do, violence may result because they are bored. For example, some people like to start fights for amusement. When children are not busy, it is easier for them to get in trouble than when they are.  Another serious consequence of not having anything positive to do is gang affiliation, which we will talk about more in depth.

## Gang Affiliation

As we mentioned before, violence is a typical thing in the world, but a big reason revealed from our experiences and what some of the survey respondents said is because grown men and women and even children are in gangs and that is what makes this world so violent. It all starts when a child is very young and they become so deep into "the game" that there is no turning back. One reason why people are in gangs is because it is a tradition in a family. Other reasons children join the gang life is because children are not given enough love and attention at home and so they see the gang as being a family. It is the closest feeling they have to love. It is also because they look to the gang for protection. When kids see how much authority and connections are available in a gang, they will do whatever it takes to survive this world and get money, pride, confidence, and strength. It makes them feel that once they are in it, and they are feared and that no one will bother or hurt them. Also, if no one is encouraging them to do well at home, there is encouragement in the gang (often to do bad) and these lost children are going to feed into that. They are really just vulnerable and are confused about what they want. They really just want help. When you think about the violent gangbangers, remember that those in a gang can be in as much pain, and have gone through as much or more, as those that are the victims of gangs.

In this section, we reviewed different reasons why people are violent. There are a lot of reasons why people are violent. It might be because they do not know how to be any other way. It may be the only way for them to deal with anger and missing love. Or, it might be their way of surviving this world, even though they are really making the world worse. These are also vicious cycles, but with the right people, we can come together and get through life without violence.

*How do you feel violence can be solved in your community?*

Another question we asked was "Write out how you feel violence can be solved in your community." Based upon the responses, we came up with three main categories. These categories are: criminal justice/law; outreach programs; and, individual choices.

The first category was criminal justice/law, which basically included anything with the police or making of the laws. Thirteen people that took the survey felt that better criminal justice is needed to eliminate violence in the community. Some of the responses included: "confiscation of drugs and weapons," "removal of liquor stores in communities," "change curfew for kids," "more intense punishment for criminals," and "increased police patrol." All of the suggested ideas can definitely benefit the elimination of violence in the community. However, no matter how more intense criminal punishment is or how many laws are made, people are always going to feel that the criminal justice system needs to be better. Sure, it is far from perfect, but maybe the reason there is so much violence is because programs that can help people—not just punish them—are not available.

The next category was "outreach", which basically includes any response that suggested some type of help and/or awareness through a group or program. Thirteen people felt such programs could eliminate violence in the community. People responded by saying: "creating more youth and anger management programs," "getting people the help they need," "talk it out," "have rallies," and "have nonviolence marches." Outreach programs can give children and adults the support that they have yearned for, but have not gotten. They can teach people about things they have never learned or heard of, such as nonviolent conflict resolution. Rallies and marches fit into this category because those types of events reach out to everyone in the community to take a stand on violence. Outreach programs do exactly what their name suggests: they reach out to people to give them places where they can become better people overall. The better and healthier people are, the less likely they are to be violent. The programs also reach out to the community to care about all of its members.

The last category was "individual choices." To be a part of this category, the responses talked about individual people making decisions, which include the person's "common sense" and prior knowledge that can be used to avoid violence. These responses included: "stop killing," "stay off the streets," "no mob violence," "using the great equalizer [one's brain]," and "just getting to know everybody." In this category, people felt that responsibility was really on the individual person to make better choices. We feel that it is a lot harder to stop violence than just telling people to "act right" and "use your brain." We have to keep in mind all of the reasons that people are violent that were reviewed in the last section and take the right action based on those reasons.

This chapter was written to include more opinions about violence in our society by surveying other teens in our community. We hope this got readers thinking about how serious a problem violence is. Also, we hope this helps readers think about why they might be involved in violent situations and what they can do to help children grow up to be caring and peaceful. We offer a lot more suggestions on how to replace violence with compassion, respect, inspiration, motivation, and empathy in the following chapter.

# PART TWO

TRAILING BEHIND
BY DESIREE TELLIS

*Stop lookin' back*
*Movin' ahead*
*Everything that happened in the past is dead*
*It can't be changed, it can't be erased*
*Yet what happens can still be traced*
*Traced in the head, traced in the mind*
*Yet the opportunity to change it lies behind.*
*Left, trailing far away*
*As the years increase day by day*
*Moving on, but the past left trailing behind.*
*Moving on, but memories still in the mind*
*Moving forward, but keep looking back*
*Moving forward, but still see the prints of the tracks*
*The tracks left behind, the tracks left trailing.*
*Those are those tracks of failing*
*In the front of the tracks I envision someone succeeding*
*Someone leaving those tracks left behind*
*Taking a new path, takin' a new way.*
*So when the eyes look back the past has no trace[1].*

---

1       This poem ties into compassion in that sometimes as people
we find it hard to care for people who have horrible pasts. However
this poem helps us to see that peoples past cannot be changed and
they cannot be traced so we need to look at the new person that they
are.

HOW FAR YOU GO IN LIFE DEPENDS ON YOUR BEING
TENDER WITH THE YOUNG, COMPASSIONATE WITH THE AGED,
SYMPATHETIC WITH THE STRIVING AND TOLERANT OF THE
WEAK AND STRONG. BECAUSE SOMEDAY IN LIFE YOU WILL
HAVE BEEN ALL OF THESE.

—GEORGE WASHINGTON CARVER

# CHAPTER 4: REPLACING VIOLENCE WITH COMPASSION, RESPECT, INSPIRATION, MOTIVATION, AND EMPATHY

THE C.R.I.M.E. TEENS

---

### COMPASSION IS:

- Love
- Sympathy
- Empathy
- Fairness
- Believing in someone
- Kindness
- Caring
- Forgiveness

---

Compassion is an important element in life because without it you aren't able to show empathy and understanding for others' situations. It is important to teach about compassion because with it, you can avoid violence and create successful solutions to a problem. The purpose of this chapter is to teach you, the adults and parents, how to explain to children the importance and benefits of having compassion.

According to Merriam-Webster.com, *compassion* is defined as, "sympathetic consciousness of others' distress together with a desire to alleviate it." But what does that mean?

Sᴍᴩᴀᴛʜᴇᴛɪᴄ Cᴏɴsᴄɪᴏᴜsɴᴇss ᴏғ Oᴛʜᴇʀs' Dɪsᴛʀᴇss Tᴏɢᴇᴛʜᴇʀ ᴡɪᴛʜ ᴀ Dᴇsɪʀᴇ ᴛᴏ Aʟʟᴇᴠɪᴀᴛᴇ Iᴛ:

From this, we conclude compassion is a complicated topic to explore. But, let's give it a try. To be *sympathetic* means to care for someone else's thoughts and feelings. *Consciousness* is your mental ability to decide what's right and what's wrong and to be aware of the situation in front of you. Consciousness involves your mind, spirit and emotions. Your mind tells you how to react to someone else or your own pain or suffering. Your spirituality helps you to be more understanding towards someone else's circumstances. If you have faith in God, you can use Him as a guide for your life decisions. If your faith is in people, you trust that they will make the right choices. Your emotions allow you to connect with the feelings of another person. So, then, when you have a mindful, spiritual, and emotional awareness of someone's distress, compassion means you try to alleviate, or help, the distress. This can be just talking to them, giving advice, or actually doing something to help make their situation easier.

Compassion can be pretty easy when it is someone you really care about and they are in a situation beyond their control, such as being laid off work or being hurt in a car accident. But, there are many times when it is *really, really* hard to show compassion. Think about the times you were judgmental and angry and missed out on seeing the suffering of someone.

## Wʜᴇɴ Cᴏᴍᴩᴀssɪᴏɴ Is Hᴀʀᴅ ᴛᴏ Fɪɴᴅ

When someone has wronged you or someone you love, we must return to the definition by making ourselves aware of others' suffering for us to be able to feel compassion. We can see then that their suffering has caused them to make bad decisions—sometimes, decisions that hurt us. In order to relieve someone else's suffering, we want to give them good criticism and understand their reason for making bad choices.

CASE EXAMPLE: FINDING COMPASSION IN A TRAGIC SITUATION
BY TIARA OUSLEY

*"In September 2009, Derrion Albert, a 16-year-old honors student was beaten to death on Chicago's Southside. Albert was walking home from school and was swept into a violent fight where he was struck in the head with a piece of wood. He later died as a result of the injuries from the beating. The fight he encountered was between two groups of teens that were from different neighborhoods; Derrion was not involved in the dispute in any way. He was a bystander to a violent act that went too far and his death was the result of an escalated incident of teen violence"* (Banchero & Mack, 2009).

So, let us reflect on this incident. We believe that although those teens beat that boy to death, it is possible to show compassion for the attackers. However, it is a challenge. When you hear something like that, it is very easy to become opinionated and judgmental as we are imperfect humans and have a mind of our own. Now those teenage boys are responsible for the death and it is difficult to see things from their point of view and forgive them. But, they are imperfect and they made a horrible mistake so, that is when you have to become compassionate towards them.

They may have had the ability to distinguish right from wrong but it is more complicated than just saying, "They should have known better." They regret it now or they will regret it later because they are living the consequences of their actions and now many people who read about this have labeled them as "animals." If you can make a stupid or horrible mistake, is it not possible to be compassionate towards them and forgive them? Those boys may have their own minds, but they could have been led on and sometimes when we are led on, it is easy to fall victim to dumb choices. When someone is messing with your mind, your mentality can be changed.

Also, the neighborhood the teens lived in and their life experiences could have led them to that particular moment that made them criminals. When a person has been around negativity for so long, eventually a caring mentality will start giving up and start feeding into the violence. Some of those teens may have never had emotional help and when their emotions are in a danger zone, they respond violently. So, although those teens did what is, sadly, a part of everyday life, you have to learn to forgive and be compassionate, because holding grudges could have a negative effect on your mentality. You could end up doing something worse (by retaliating) or your character can change unconsciously to become negative and hostile because you decided not to become compassionate towards them.

62 |

### Role Models Who Exemplify Compassion

In this section, we highlight three famous individuals that we feel really showed compassion. We recommend you talk to your kids and students about these individuals. Talk about what they do/did and also the *values* that they live(d) by.

#### Oprah Winfrey

Oprah is the mother of all role models because she expresses compassion very deeply and she never lets money block the way of her thinking because she always gives it back to those in need. She built a school in Africa that children can attend for free. She knew that with the right tools and education, the children will be able to have a successful and bright future. Oprah has been able to cover a wide array of subjects dealing with violence. She has been able to talk about dating and domestic violence and so forth. One specific example of Oprah helping others to prevent violence is when she had a show that was discussing *A Parent's Guide to Teen Dating Violence.* This book basically was helping parents to talk to their kids about their relationships and how to prevent violence.

## MARTIN LUTHER KING JR.

Martin Luther King Jr. exemplified compassion because he went beyond the limits during his time trying to make change and extended his hand to everyone (including his racist enemies) to make the world a more caring, peaceful, and just place. He was a civil rights leader and without his accomplishments, it would be even harder for the roles models today to make a change. Not only did Martin Luther King raise awareness about violence, but he also helped people to see that violence is not the way. Martin did this with a very powerful quote, "Returning violence for violence multiplies violence, adding deeper darkness to a night already devoid of stars... Hate cannot drive out hate: only love can do that." This statement is very true in today's society. Most people do the opposite of this statement and they return violence for violence and for years these problems have never been taken care of.

## ABRAHAM LINCOLN

Abraham Lincoln is important to the African American community because without him a lot of African Americans would not have any freedom and things may be the same for this population. Not even Obama would be president today if it were not for Abraham Lincoln. He allowed African Americans to set goals and accomplish them and that has benefited America as well as a greater society. Abraham Lincoln showed compassion when he recognized that blacks were more than 3/5's of a person. He realized that they were whole people just like whites and other nationalities that existed in those days. Abraham Lincoln showed compassion to the Blacks despite the possibility of people within his own race turning against him. It can truly be said that he showed compassion.

## COMPASSION IN EVERYDAY LIFE

In this section, we took turns writing about the compassion we have experienced or seen in our everyday lives and talk about how a little bit of compassion may prevent violence.

## EXAMPLE #1

A time when I experienced compassion was when I was downtown at McDonald's by Loyola and a homeless man asked me for 10 cents. I gave it to him and he asked to give me a kiss. Of course I said "no" and just said, "You're welcome." I learned that by doing the littlest things for people in need can mean a lot. If people show compassion some people will be less likely to go out and commit violence, kill, or rob because they feel as if they are cared for.

## EXAMPLE #2

There was a time a group of people were messing with this girl in my neighborhood. They said a few things that were really bad like, "You're ugly, fat, and tall." So I went to her and asked her if she was okay. She said "yes," but I took her up to my house and gave her some food. Then I told her when she went home to make sure she didn't talk to any strangers. I made sure she got on the bus and learned that it is okay to help others. What I learned in this situation was to treat people how I want to be treated because if that had happened to me, I would have wanted someone to help me. This may have stopped a potential fight if she tried to get back at the group making fun of her.

## Example #3

A time when I experienced compassion is when I was at church; a homeless man came in and was saying that he didn't have much and sometimes nothing. At that time, I was thinking how I felt sorry for him and if I could have done something, I would have. The reason I couldn't help him was because I was a teenager and the adults had to take over because he was a stranger. The homeless person did get help. If more people could help and show compassion, the others would not commit a crime.

## Example #4

A person that shows compassion would be my grandma because she shows sympathy for others. When my grandma sees that something is wrong, she will just reach out and do the best she can. An example is when my sister and I were little, she showed compassion by raising my sister and me to be nice and respectful young adults when our parents were not available. My grandma shows compassion for a lot of things but what she taught us I will never forget. I will use the compassion she taught us, if I have kids later in life, and then I can teach them from my experiences.

## Example #5

A person that shows compassion is my pastor. He reaches out to people that are struggling and who do not have anything. He comes to church on a daily basis to different events and also takes the time to go over his sermon to people who may not have fully understood it. Also my pastor will call the sick to see if they are ok. My pastor works to prevent violence by setting up different activities after school. He started a boys step team and later let the girls have a step team.

### ADVICE FOR TEACHERS

- Listen to concerns.
  - **Example:** If a student comes to a teacher and is concerned about his/her grade in the class, the teacher can go over missing assignments and make sure that the student understands all of the material.
- Be considerate.
  - **Example:** If your student feels sick or there seems like they are having problems, talk to them. Recommend places where they can get help like the school nurse, guidance counselor, or social worker.
- Avoid sarcasm.
  - **Example:** If your student asks you a question and you already had given directions, do not repeat them in a sarcastic way. The student might feel afraid to ask other questions in the future.
- Show that you are not there only to lecture and grade your students.
  - **Example:** Care about the students' improvement in other classes other than the ones you teach them in. Help them become all around better students.
- Reach out to students having problems.
  - **Example:** Show interest in students who have a

hard time learning or have discipline problems; there might be something underneath these issues.

- Incorporate activities in the class that teach compassion
  - **Example**: Perform a skit where kids and teens take on different roles to see what it is like to be someone in need and how they would help.
  - **Example**: Teachers can have open discussions about violence and how they feel about what is going on in the community. If talking about crime, help the students see the perspectives of the offender and the victim.

## Advice for Parents

- Do not be lazy.
  - **Example**: Go to places with your kids. Teach them about their communities and neighbors. Also, help kids in the house set a standard. Care for them by working on things like chores together.
- Ease up; soften your heart; do not be so strict.
  - **Example**: You do not necessarily always have to punish your kids with spankings. Instead sit and talk with them about what they did wrong and work together on a way to solve the problem.
- Be a parent, not a friend.
  - **Example**: Love your child and know what is going on in their life. But you cannot act like a teenager. Otherwise, kids might not understand the boundaries between kids and parents. This will teach children to be compassionate toward their elders.
- Do not put your child down.

- **Example**: Putting your child down will not teach them to be compassionate toward others. This will set an example for a child to put other people down instead of trying to help and care for them.
- Be optimistic, do not be so stressed.
  - **Example**: Take time to relax after a stressful situation so that you avoid taking stress out on your kids. This will help kids learn how to manage their stress as well.
- Teach your kids to care for others.
  - **Example**: You can show that you care for others. Help get your kids involved in activities that use community service. Also, parents can get involved in volunteering in their kids' lives, like schools or religious institutions.
- Understand kids are kids.
  - Kids are learning how life works. Do not expect things from us that we may not know how to do.
- Show you care about your child by spending time with him or her.
  - **Example**: Family game night. Some kids get mad when they lose a game. Just talk to them when they get upset. It should be about playing, not winning!
  - **Example**: Saying "I love you" shows you care. Some people stray away from saying it.
  - **Example**: Parents should have AT LEAST one daily check-in and one lengthy weekly conversation with their kids.

## ADVICE FOR THE MEDIA

- Turn to more positive stories.
    - **Example**: Show what celebrities or citizens are doing to help. For example, STCU was a story about musicians who were singing at a benefit to increase awareness for cancer research.
- Stop gossiping about celebrities.
    - **Example**: Websites like Perez Hilton's make fun of people's suffering. Remember to "treat others how you would want to be treated." Show compassion for celebrities that are having problems.
- Limit violence.
    - **Example**: There are more movies about violence than compassion. This sets a tone for a more violent society.
    - **Example**: In video games, Accentuate other skills besides killing people when developing video games.
- Avoid stereotypes and prejudice against different groups.
    - **Example**: Use the media as a way to show what we have in common and help build compassion to individuals that face challenges or discrimination (i.e., people in poverty, homosexuals).
- The media can show compassion by having a show or sitcom with a dramatic plot where the main character will show compassion.
    - **Example**: Law and Order SVU has characters (police, investigators, and lawyers) whom are showing compassion toward children and women who experience violent acts against them.

- Some examples of shows that are not
  compassionate are: the dating shows on
  VH1, Jersey Shore, and Dr. Phil (sometimes).

## A Dignity Stolen
### by Desiree Tellis

As these days move along, respect diminishes
No longer here, no longer existing
Loved one's beaten, hearts bleeding, children broken,
dignity stolen.
No respect, no love, where's the respect we used to love
Where's the respect we used to cherish
Where's the respect that used to be embellished
Embellished in our minds, engraved in our hearts
Where's the respect that should have been taught to us
from the start
Where's the respect that we should experience
When you don't know respect, you don't know when you're
being disrespected
Respect is what helps us learn life lessons
We hope, we wish, we want, we need respect to return
We need to erase these burns of disrespect in society
We need to remove all this anxiety
If there were respect, there wouldn't have to be hard life
lessons to learn
So remember respect, engrave it in your heart
And you can make the road you take in life not so hard

RESPECT FOR OURSELVES GUIDES OUR MORALS—RESPECT FOR OTHERS GUIDES OUR MANNERS.

—LAURENCE STERNE

| RESPECT IS: |
| --- |
| • Loyalty |
| • Receiving and giving– respect goes both ways |
| • Treat people the way you want to be treated |
| • Self-love |
| • Love of others |
| • Respect to authority and peers |
| • Esteem (self and others) |
| • Fulfill your obligations to someone else |

Many times violence starts because someone feels that they have been disrespected. People react on their first impulse. When you are consistently respectful to others, it makes it more difficult for them to disrespect you or you to act violently. In order to receive respect, you must respect others. In this chapter, we will discuss how to prevent violence with respect.

But what does that mean? According to the Oxford University Press **respect** is "deferential esteem felt or shown toward a person or quality." What does THAT mean?

It means giving value to another's beliefs, morals, personalities, preferences, and differences. For instance, if someone doesn't believe in eating pork, but you do, it would be most respectful to accept his or her choice. However it is okay to ask, or to want to learn more about another's perspective. Two individuals may have differing moral views because of how they look at the consequences. Even though there may be consequences, they still need to respect the person's point of view. We should respect that everyone has a different personality. You can be respectful by accepting others' shortcomings. Everyone has flaws. Lastly, respect others' preferences; for example, discrimination is common toward homosexuals. So, a person might be attracted to someone of the same sex and you may disagree with the action, but you should still treat them with respect.

Being respectful does not mean sitting back or feeding off of other people's negativity. You can be respectful and still speak up in an inoffensive way. You can use diplomacy and choose your words carefully. Be open-minded and open-hearted.

We want to make on final distinction. There is a difference between respect and being respectful. Being respectful means to act positively toward the person and to be courteous, considerate, and helpful. Respect, on the other hand, must be earned. So, you can be respectful even if someone has not earned your respect. Whether or not someone has earned your respect is a reflection on them; being respectful is a reflection of *YOU*.

### ROLE MODELS WHO EXEMPLIFY RESPECT

In this section, we highlight three famous individuals that we feel really show(ed) respect. We recommend you talk to your kids and students about these individuals. Talk about what they do and also the *values* that they live(d) by.

### MOTHER TERESA

Mother Teresa had a general respect for the value of human life and constantly put others before herself. She provided support for the sick, needy and underprivileged. She valued everyone's health and did not judge anyone. She wanted everyone to be happy and to be successful. She gave others the chance to continue living instead of just forgetting about them. Respect is not just to treat people of a certain material or social stature well, but it is to treat those of all social classes equally. It is founded on the basis of equality, justice, and kindness.

### 9/11 RESPONSE CREW

The 9/11 response crew put their lives on the line for the safety and well being of others during the terrorist attacks. These individuals saved other peoples' lives instead of looking out for themselves. These men and women were very courageous and showed a lot of respect for human life. They gave as many people as possible a chance to see another day and to see their families, friends and loved ones. Not only did the 9/11 crew help those who were in the building, but they also helped those who were on the streets and anyone who may have been around. The 9/11 response crew set a good example in not returning evil with evil. They put their energy into helping those that needed help at that point in time.

## Beyoncé

Beyoncé is very caring and can be a great friend. Although she maybe busy, she always makes time to support others. She gives full attention to various charitable organizations. Another example of her showing respect is when she visited someone who was hurt during one of her concerts in the hospital, which showed that she really wanted to make sure that they were okay. She also showed a great deal of respect for Taylor Swift at the MTV Video Music Awards. Whereas Kanye West was verbally and emotionally violent by interrupting and putting down Taylor when she won an award (beating Beyoncé), Beyoncé showed respect for Taylor as an artist and a person by giving Taylor her speaking time later that night at the awards.

## Respect in Everyday Life

Here are some examples of respect seen in everyday life. We hope people see how by simply respecting others and oneself, all violence can be stopped.

## Example #1

There was a time when I was faced with a situation that almost forced me to be disrespectful toward an elderly woman. I was on the CTA bus one day on my way home. I was listening to my IPOD and looking out the window. An elderly lady got on the bus, sat next to me and began to sing so loud I heard her over my music. I asked her politely to lower her voice. But instead of her lowering her voice, she sang louder and moved closer toward me. Because I showed respect, I did not say anything and I moved to another seat. She could have been having a bad day, so instead of having a big argument or confrontation, I just let it go because I was always taught to respect my elders. With this being said, always consider the reaction to your actions and choose your battles wisely.

## Advice for Teachers
- Be open-minded; respect is not a one-way street.
  - Treat your students how you want to be treated; if you want them to listen to you, listen to them.
  - **Example**: If you want them to be quiet, do not say "shut up" or yell; model.
- Teach your students how to respect diverse opinions and beliefs through discussions.
  - **Example**: When talking about topics that are controversial like religion, allow all students to discuss their opinions. Students should be allowed to express themselves in a nonjudgmental space.
  - Understand the limitations of your own beliefs. Recognize opinions from facts; do not be biased in how you teach.
- Respect your students' views on how to best learn. Ask for and accept criticism about your teaching.

## Advice for Parents
- Do not just look at yourself as "the boss;" it is

the way how you say things. We do not think you
should have to beg your kids to do things, but
please do not curse or yell. Talk to them like how
you expect them to talk to you. It does not make
sense to punish your child for swearing if you are
always yelling and swearing at them.
- Give a reason why you are asking your kids to do
  things—NOT "Because I said so"; have them think
  about the effects of doing what you ask them.
- Listen to kids' opinions; it might not be right, but
  you can see what they think about things.
  - **Example**: If a kid wants more freedom and
    wants to stay out late the parent might
    not want them to because they feel their
    kids will be unsafe. Explain this to kids
    and listen to your kids' opinions about the
    situation. Kids might not understand exactly
    where a parent is coming from and parents
    might not understand where kids are
    coming from. There might need to be a more
    in depth discussion about a disagreement.

## ADVICE TO THE MEDIA
- Some news doesn't give you all the facts
  - **Example**: Some news shows only give facts
    from their perspective. They might not take
    into account values of their entire audience.
- The media can stop making African American
  communities look scary and out-of-control. Black
  communities are not the only places where
  violence occurs. Also, there are many more
  nonviolent African Americans than violent ones.
- Stop tearing down celebrities
  - **Example**: Look at any tabloid or celebrity
    blog and you will see gossip about Britney

Spears, Miley Cyrus, and Lindsey Lohan. It makes celebrities feel bad because what is being said might not necessarily be true. It also sets an example for disrespect from the people who are reading the news stories about them.

## Our Past Generations' Forgotten Pain and Cries
### by Tiara Ousley

*We fancy those who twirl into fame*
*But we forget about those that have fought for our days*
*We look at ourselves and see no shame*
*Because we've forgotten imperfect role models that have*
*faded*
*We obsess over beauty and forget about what's important*
*And let distortion take its course into true beauty's lies*
*But what about our past generations' pain and cries*
*But we stay selfish and let their motivations diminish*
*It seems that few like Obama, Winfrey, and Banks are the*
*vestige of slave's hopes and dreams*
*How are we to keep these dreams alive*
*When we forget about our past generations' pain and cries*
*A ugly turn has begun*
*But as more change comes about*
*The more time diverges into something more negative*
*When will we step it up for hope*
*Not just when Obama makes it as the first black president*
*of America*
*But when will we stop being cowards and stop letting the*
*racists define who we are and what we're going to turn*
*out to be*
*When are we going to stop hurting ourselves, letting pride*
*get in the way?*
*When are we going to start being selfless and stop letting*
*our past generation's dreams decay?*
*And when are we going to stop letting our courage hide?*

FAILURE IS TAKING THE PATH THAT EVERYONE ELSE DOES.
SUCCESS IS MAKING YOUR OWN PATH.

—UNKNOWN

INSPIRATION IS:

- Role models – people you look up to
- Good influences
- A good feeling that motivates you
- Creative ideas
- Energy
- Idolization
- Believing in someone – Believing in yourself
- Confidence

According to thefreedictionary.com, inspiration is "stimulation of the mind or emotions to a high level of feeling or activity." According to dictionary.com, inspiration is defined as "an animating action or influence."

In other words, inspiration is someone or something that influences you or another person to strive for better. Inspiration is a quality that everyone needs throughout their lives. With inspiration, you have an extra driving force to make you want to take whatever you are doing to the next level. For some people, this is all they need to be better in life. They might not have enough love and care at home.

Even just a little bit of inspiration might help some people get out of their current situation. When inspiration comes into the picture it can take people's minds off of obstacles, such as current living conditions or what is happening in their neighborhood. Inspiration can encourage someone want to be better in life as opposed to going out in the world and committing a crime. As teens in the C.R.I.M.E. project, we have been inspired by different role models in our lives and we hope to start an "inspiration cycle," where we try and inspire youth to reach their goals; then, when they get older, we hope they will continue the cycle.

### Role Models That Exemplify Inspiration

In this section, we highlight three famous individuals that are inspiring. We recommend parents and adults talk to kids and students about these individuals. Talk about what they do and also the *values* that they live(d) by.

### Madame C.J. Walker

This amazing woman had come from rags to riches and because of her success, people now can enjoy great hair. When she was a little girl, she did not really get the chance to get a proper education, due to the legislators refusing to give funds for the black children in schools in Louisiana. Madame Walker did not let that break her; she improved her reading and writing skills and became a successful businesswoman. With her accomplishments, other African American women are encouraged to rise above adversity and persevere. Madame C.J. Walker's example can teach violence prevention in that it demonstrates that if you are poor, you do not have to steal, but you can do like she did and make something out of your life.

### Rosa Parks

Mrs. Parks is an outstanding, courageous woman. She protested on a bus in order to do the simplest thing in the world: to sit anywhere on the bus. The outcome of her action is now a right that African Americans have today. This beautiful lady won the Peace Abbey Courage of Conscience Award, and now there are many Americans and other nations' citizens following her example to fight for their rights and the rights of others. Although people are fighting for their rights, most need to do it in a nonviolent way. People do not need to use violence when they are trying to overcome oppression, but they can simply use their voices, skills, knowledge, and common sense.

## REVEREND RUN

One famous person that is also inspiring is Reverend Run. Rev Run started as a rapper in a group called Run D.M.C. He has a cable television show called *Run's House*. This show is about him and his family. One thing that is so inspiring about Rev Run is that he is close to his family and helps with everything they need. At the end of each episode, Rev Run inspires others by sending an important message, such as: "Look for the GOOD in the people in your life. Don't be a excessive complainer. (Remember) A faultfinder will find faults in paradise! God is Love, Rev Run." From these positive messages we learn to help our families as well as anybody who needs help.

## BOOKER T. WASHINGTON

Booker T. Washington was an inspiration because he overcame the odds by becoming an educated Black man in a time when most Americans did not see the intellectual potential of African Americans. He was an educator and an advocate for education for everyone—regardless of their race or social status. We need to recognize him and see what the minds of African Americans can discover and create in this world.

## INSPIRATION IN EVERYDAY LIFE

The following are examples of times the CRIME project authors have been inspired or seen others inspired. We believe that if kids and teens are inspired to do achieve greatness in their lives, violence will not be an option for them.

EXAMPLE #1

Being a teen can sometimes cause you to make a lot of wrong decisions. We become so caught up in what is going on around us that we do not think about what is right or wrong. That is why it is good to have someone that is really an inspiration in our lives. For me, my step mom is my inspiration. She goes through a lot and she continues to push forward. She never lets what anybody says or assumes about her get in the way. She goes on with life because she knows there are bigger things to worry about. This inspires me to do the same. I get through life a lot better with her wise decisions and words. Her style of conviction could help prevent violence in the future because if anybody ever worries about what someone says about them and avoids it, the conflict will be avoided as well.

EXAMPLE #2

I can think of many positive people that inspire me, but I also turn to negative people for inspiration. Although people can act ignorant, I don't judge them. They teach me through their actions to not respond negatively because the only thing that it will lead to is violence. When people are very rude to me, they are really displaying a silent message to me saying this is not the true way to act. Basically they inspire and teach me to always behave in a well-mannered way. The Dalai Lama said, "In the practice of tolerance, one's enemy's the best teacher."

EXAMPLE #3

Someone who I find inspirational is a professor named Dr. Crawley (a professor at the School of Social Work at Loyola). She inspired me when she spoke to our after school program because of the things she said. I really cannot recall what it was in particular, but I can remember how she made me feel. I know she talked about the importance of education and how no matter what disadvantages we have to deal with, we have "the great equalizer"—that is, our mind. I felt so inspired to improve my whole being, to change, and to do better in life. Dr. Crawley got me thinking on a whole new level, like a whole new world had opened up to me. In this world is reality, reality of positive energy. She made me think more logically about what I wanted to do in life. It was not just what she said it was her spunky personality that really got me listening to her. She did not care what anyone thought of her and she was really fun to talk to. She was funny and that made the discussion lighthearted in a serious way.

After her powerful words, I now take the time to think and reflect on the decisions I make every day. I think about the world and how she mentioned to explore and how my dreams could fit into reality without just being a dream. An unseen world would leave you locked in your environment, comfortable, away from the opportunities and growth that exist in your life. I do not want to miss that, so the only way to clarify and beautify my life is to explore. If we do not explore, we will miss out on the great accomplishments that are ahead. I do not want to miss out on those explorations, because through them someone could find me inspiring. Hey! That is the circle of life.

That inspirational moment with Dr. Crawley has made me more open minded. If everyone could explore the world and experience the same, than people would be less violent. Violence would decrease because people would view the world and each other in a positive perspective. If a person's mentality is changed positively, a person's emotional state experiences the same effect. A person would have second thoughts about committing violent acts. Most acts of violence start in the mind. With a new outlook, violence is less likely be the outcome of a situation. The point of this example is that the moment of inspiration may be temporary but the feelings will always remain, and that is what people need to experience.

## ADVICE TO TEACHERS

- Recognize the little things that students do and inspire them to continue to do them.
    - **Example:** If a student always turns in his/her homework, let the student know that you appreciate that he/she is organized and disciplined.
- Take an interest in students' lives.
    - **Example:** If you have students who are on the basketball team and are dedicated to sports, you could attend some of their games to support them outside of school.

- Help students understand that in order to succeed there will also be times when they might fail, but to never give up.
    - **Example:** If tests are really difficult and students get bad grades, teachers can encourage them to do well in other areas like in their research papers to increase their grade.
- Make classroom assignments inspiring.
    - **Example:** Draw a comic of yourself ten years from now.
    - **Example:** Research a hero or someone who inspires you.
- Share inspiring stories with students (strong women, African American history, etc.).
    - **Example:** There was a teacher who told us about when he went to college. There was a

lot of material that he had never learned. He took it upon himself to study even harder to catch up to the other students.

## ADVICE TO PARENTS

- Be supportive of your children's positive goals.
    - **Example**: If your child is in an extracurricular activity like band, make a point to attend their concerts.
- Make a collage of pictures with your child relating to their goals and dreams. Give advice on how to move towards their goals. If you are not knowledgeable on how they can accomplish their goals, partner with them to get answers.
- Support your child's dreams.
    - **Example**: Get a sketchbook for your artistic child and have him/her try to be the next Picasso!
- Do not compare your kids to each other; they have different personalities and interests.
    - **Example**: Some kids might be good at sports, some might be good at school. Take an interest in the separate skills that kids have and help them be inspired to succeed.

## ADVICE TO THE MEDIA

- Include more positive news about successful kids; there is so much negative news.
    - **Examples**: Create more networks like Nickelodeon and PBS Kids.
    - **Think about this**: How many times have you turned off a program because of something positive?
- Feature celebrities doing charity rather than exploiting their mistakes.

- **Examples**: Michael Jackson (pre-death), Angelina Jolie, Beyonce, Wyclef Jean, Alicia Keys
- **Think about this**: How would you feel if everyone knew your mistakes?
- Air more commercials for learning centers or youth programs/activities.
- Show more advertising outlining the benefits of college.
- Try to feature shows with more qualities like the Oprah Show.
  - **Examples**: Compassion, Inspiration, being empathic to others, understanding people's feelings and different perspectives.
  - **Think about this**: Do you think talk shows that encourage guest to be violent like Jerry Springer and Maury Povich, help or hurt our society?

## STEPPING UP FOR HOPE
### BY TIARA OUSLEY

Hope is a disappointment
It feels dead it's always a lie
Every time you hold on to it
It falls; it's always going to die
We feel that life will always remain the same
Misfortunes hit us so we look for someone to blame
For all those times that we have cried
We think to ourselves that hope was never alive
We pray to God because ain't hope his word, his voice, his
phrase
The Holy God we supposedly praise
We get so angry when things don't go our way
So we forget about God until hope starts to fade
We should take some part in making hope come true
Instead of procrastinating and waiting for it to come out
of the blue
How can we pray to God and expect him to do all we
desire
When **we** can make things happen
Instead of putting him to blame and calling him a liar
If you dream it or picture it, then make it come alive
If you want it
Get out of your shell and stop trying to hide
If you want God to answer your prayers then you have to
take your part
He will realize you want it and that's when hope will start
Stop going to the bible just because life begins to turn
If you only do it for that then hope will surely burn

SHOOT FOR THE MOON. EVEN IF YOU MISS, YOU'LL LAND
AMONG THE STARS.

— BRIAN LITRELL

## MOTIVATION IS:

- Taking action
- Feeling energized
- Feeling welcome
- Being encouraged
- Overcoming obstacles
- Achievement
- Rewards
- Exciting
- Being interested
- Something that drives you

According to dictionary.com, *motivation* is "to provide with an incentive; move to action; impel." Motivation is when something or someone pushes another to reach for his/her dreams and goals. Dreams and goals are simply what people want to accomplish in life. One way to motivate is to push someone to accomplish something with your actions or words. Motivating someone can create a big change in his or her future because they know that another person cares. At times, that is all a person really needs. It is often okay to work alone, but it is even better to have a partner by your side that will encourage you to keep striving forward. Motivation is important because a little stimulation can create a foundation for others to do the unexpected, meaning they will achieve what they never thought they could. It forces innovation and forms a positive change in one's self.

Motivation could benefit a person when dealing with violence because then a person might take time out to consider what would be the right response. If the person is motivated by positive future goals, he/she will be less likely to be pulled into a negative or violent situation. It is important to motivate in positive ways, like giving encouragement or finding out about a kid's dreams, and not threatening them or trying to scare them with comments like "You're gonna end up like your daddy in jail."

## Role Models That Exemplify Motivation
Following are some role models that show an unbelievable amount of motivation in achieving their success and they use their words and positions to motivate young people.

### Barack Obama
Barack Obama is one of the greatest role models that has ever walked this earth. He is to us what Martin Luther King Jr. was in his day. He became America's first African American president, which was the biggest accomplishment for African Americans to date. He won the Nobel Peace Prize award for "extraordinary efforts to strengthen international diplomacy and cooperation between peoples" (http://www.cnn.com/2009/WORLD/europe/10/09/nobel.peace.prize/index.html). He constantly tries to motivate everyone to CHANGE, to get involved, and to be the best that they can. Many of us were motivated by his address to the students in America on the first day of school in 2009. We recommend that adults find it online and share it with the children in your life.

### Tyler Perry
Tyler is a very talented man who used his talents to succeed. He worked very hard to get to the top, and now he is a millionaire movie director. He lived in his car for years and never stopped pursuing his dreams. Because of his determination, he is now one of the most recognized entertainment professionals. Most people today who think they do not have enough resources feel that they have

to steal, but Tyler Perry did not do that. Instead, Mr. Perry actively pursued his dreams. Everyone's situation may not turn out like his, but by staying motivated, everyone can accomplish at least some of their goals.

## Sonia Sotomayor

Sonia Sotomayor became the first Hispanic and third woman to be a justice on the U.S. Supreme Court. She is a very determined woman who excelled in school and was once a professor at New York University. She is a very positive influence on Hispanics and other minority groups who worked her way toward her destiny. Now she shines very brightly in fulfilling her duties as one of the leaders of the Supreme Court. Sonia Sotomayor motivates people to strive for their goals and to keep hope alive. By keeping hope alive, people will not have to resort to violence; they may not even consider violence as an option.

## Motivation in Everyday Life

The following are some of stories of motivation to show that you do not have to become President or a Supreme Court Justice to display motivation or to motivate others. On the contrary, you can be a motivating teen just like us.

## Example #1

I had an experience with motivation in my neighborhood when I was talking to people on the streets about domestic violence. I shared with those who were interested that they should treat their wives or spouses as they would their own body. They do not hit themselves so they should not hit anyone else. What I learned was that by taking the initiative to talk to people about domestic violence, I could help people to consider change if they are involved in hitting their spouses. More people have to know about this issue and get involved to prevent domestic violence.

## Example #2

I was at military school doing drills. An older teen called us to attention. The older teen wanted us to be motivated to do our drills correctly so that we can display that we care about what we are doing. The person had to motivate us by leading and helping us practice. This experience demonstrated that peers can motivate other peers. Peer motivation is important because teens are more willing to listen to each other and understand their perspective. I think that positive peer action can prevent violence when a peer is a good leader.

94 |

## Advice to Teachers

- Follow up with students.
    - **Example**: If a student is having difficulty on a paper, check in with them before it is due to make sure that they are staying on track.
- Help your students outside of class and vary your teaching techniques.
    - **Example**: Some students will not understand the material in class. You might need to help outside of class time.
    - **Example**: A good way to help them understand material better is to do different activities that are not included in your lesson plans. Also use other ways to teach material, like using music, visuals, or poetry helps students become excited about a subject.
- Be a cheerleader. "There you go! You're finally getting it!"

- **Example**: Students might respond well to teachers who encourage them verbally. Telling students that they are on the right track will let them know that you believe in them.
- **Example**: Simple things like putting smiley faces on papers can encourage students.
- Lead by example, be a role model.
  - **Example**: Be prepared. Have your lessons planned. Do your work.
- Show that you love what you teach.
  - **Example**: A teacher who is passionate about what he or she teaches makes students more motivated to learn. It seems to us that some teachers do not like their jobs or are not interested in the subjects they are teaching. We are more excited to learn when teachers are excited to help us.
- Keep students focused.
  - **Example**: Find class activities to help kids stay engaged in what you are teaching, create games or activities that keep students energized.
  - **Example**: Teach them "Where there's a will, there's a way." If you give up on them and do not help them focus on their goals, they will give up on themselves.
- Volunteer to supervise free after school programs.
- Provide students with statistics reflecting positive accomplishments by kids and teens.
  - **Example**: Show how many kids graduated from your high school or how many were successful on ACT or SAT scores. This might help kids become motivated to do better in school.

- Have the students come up with "Warrior Tasks." These are tasks that require the kid or teen to be a nonviolent warrior. They have to take a task that requires courage, such as going to a class they are failing or writing an essay they do not want to write, and work on improving in that area. Support the kids as they try to make a change in subjects or tasks that are difficult for them.
- Use field trips to inform students about history and how famous leaders stay motivated and motivated others.

## ADVICE TO PARENTS

- Ask about any homework; do not just expect them to get it done.
  - **Example**: Parents can have a set time where they will help their kids with homework. If parents do not have time to help, they can help their children find a tutor.

- If you give a compliment, do not take it away. Recognize what your child did do right.
  - **Example**: Do not tell a child that they did well on something and then right away point out the major mistakes. This might make kids feel that you only care about what they are failing in and not what they are passionate about. An example of this could be if your kid wins his/her basketball game, but is still doing poorly in school, and you immediately point this out to them.
- Remember that all kids are not the same. There are different ways to motivate kids, so you may have to do different things for your different children.
- Talk to your kids about their dreams. Help them figure out the best plan on how to get there.

- **Example**: Try to use the internet or books that will give information about what your kid wants to do. Share them with your kid and talk with them about how to best use these resources.
- Find your child a mentor in a job he/she is interested in.
- Make a time capsule of what your child sees in the future.
- DON'T motivate your kids by threatening them, such as with physical punishment, or by comparing them to someone in their family that is in jail or has been killed.

## ADVICE TO THE MEDIA
- Make music with a message; artists who use their art for a positive purpose
    - **Examples**: Common, Erykah Badu, India Arie, Maxwell, Mary J. Blige.
- Create more shows about successful people of all backgrounds and cultures.
    - **Examples**: Run's House, The Cosby Show, My Wife and Kids, Family Matters.

## Welcoming Hearts
### by Daria Siler

*In my shoes you could be*
*Just showing a little empathy*
*Understanding is all you need*
*Between the lines you could read*

*Patience is the key*
*A small conversation between you and me*
*You'll get so much more*
*And I'll have better than before*

*I can't imagine what your life is like*
*But talking can give me some insight*
*In the end I'll be able to say someone listened*
*And things will feel so much lighter*
*Then the future will become so much brighter*

*Obstacles and struggles will be broken*
*Because we'll make empathy our biggest token*

PEOPLE WILL FORGET WHAT YOU SAID. PEOPLE WILL FORGET WHAT YOU DID, BUT PEOPLE WILL NEVER FORGET HOW YOU MADE THEM FEEL.

—BONNIE JEAN WASMUND

---

### EMPATHY IS:

- Putting yourself in someone's shoes
- Seeing from another's perspective
- Caring for others
- Being understanding
- Not being judgmental
- Respecting another's opinion

---

Empathy is beyond listening to another person. It is being capable of understanding and putting yourself in others' shoes. Empathy is being able to stray away from personal feelings and giving your full attention to the other person. To pursue the use of empathy is to open your ears and listen, while putting your selfish ways aside. The importance of empathy is to let others know that you care and are listening to what they are saying, while knowing that for every person that has the same problem, his or her response will vary. If another person wants to hear from you, you may give some advice or suggestions.  But, the most important thing for you to do is listen to them before jumping in with your opinion. While the other person may benefit from your opinion or advice, he or she will get the biggest benefit by getting hardships off their chest.

| 101

Empathy is related to violence prevention. Many violent acts could be prevented through the use of empathy. The use of violence usually starts in a disagreement. Using empathy in a heated debate can create positive energy in a disagreement, allowing the two individuals to find a solution. Also, if people just had someone to talk to who really wants to learn how they feel, they will be less likely to bottle up anger and take it out on others with violent acts.

## ROLE MODELS THAT EXEMPLIFY EMPATHY

We feel that these famous individuals demonstrate empathy in their actions and so we can learn from them.

### ALICIA KEYS

Alicia expresses empathy by looking back at her experiences being a teen and growing up in a neighborhood filled with crime, prostitution, and drug dealers. She grew up in Hell's Kitchen. Now, Alicia has a whole new lifestyle but is able to empathize with children and teens who are still growing up in those harsh conditions. So, she tries to provide support to those in need and reflect upon her negative childhood experiences. She knows that it is a challenge for those to seek help and make positive changes.

### TYRA BANKS

Tyra is a role model by displaying good character when she helps others to see things from a different point of view such as lifestyles which include the following issues: religion vs. sexual orientation, race and acceptance, weight and body image, and homelessness. When Tyra does this, she loosens up the tension between others differences when it comes to disagreements about someone's lifestyle. This has affected others because they can become less violent towards someone they may dislike based upon their views.

### GHANDI

Ghandi was a spiritual leader from India who fought for both his people's rights and human rights around the world. Usually, people are only interested in helping their own race or country but he was looking out for everyone. He showed them that no matter what race you are, everyone deserve equality. He even risked his freedom for others and that showed strength as he gave himself up for the sake of others. Ghandi's approach toward social problems was always non-violent and he showed compassion and empathy for his enemy. He showed no hypocrisy. He talked about stopping violence, and he was not a doer of it himself, which could have made people more accepting to what he had to say.

## EMPATHY IN EVERYDAY LIFE
### EXAMPLE #1

There was a time when I had no other option but to show empathy toward one of my classmates. My friend and I were joking and playing around in our geometry class. He was standing next to me and he had a clipboard in his hand. I knocked it out of his hand and it landed on a girl's desk. She had received news earlier that one of her friends had died that day so when the clipboard landed on her desk, she flipped out. She picked it up and threw it across the classroom. We all got sent to the disciplinarian. In the end, our actions were dismissed and I apologized to the girl for what I had done and for her loss. I felt that if I had known about her friend, I would not have been playing around her. But I placed myself in her shoes and fully understand why she did what she did. So from this experience I learned that there is a time and place for everything, and to always place myself in someone else's shoes to understand a little better why people do the things they do and say the things they say.

### EXAMPLE #2

Empathy is when you put yourself in someone else's shoes to understand and sympathize with them. In society today, a lot of people are mainly about self-interest. They do things that only benefit them. I believe it is just another idea used to express selfishness; however, there are some people who have everybody's interest at heart. On my eleventh birthday, I wanted to go to the movies, but some of my friends didn't want to see the movie I wanted to see. They thought the movie was boring but I did not and it was my birthday. Then again they were my guests and I wanted them to enjoy themselves. So I compromised and went to see a movie everybody would enjoy. Showing empathy for others can prevent violence because empathy is just another example of compromising, because it forces people to solve an issue before it escalates into a negative situation. I learned that when you show empathy for others you can still have fun and in a way get what you actually want.

## ADVICE TO TEACHERS

- Teach children about empathy by talking about it, writing about it and practicing it.
- Show them tapes of kids their age who are less fortunate. For example a tape of kids in Africa who do not have a bed to sleep in or do not have toys to play with. Ask them what it would be like to be in their shoes.
- Teachers can relate their personal stories of how they struggled to become what they are today. This might help students to identify with teachers.
- Teachers can model empathy in the classroom. They can listen to all sides of the story to fix problems. If students are acting out, try to see why by talking to them one-on-one.
  - **Example**: Even if a student does not come to a teacher for help when he/she is struggling, the teacher should show compassion and approach the student. There are a lot reasons that students may not be doing well in a class – Don't just assume the student is "lazy" or "doesn't care."

- Break up the day with activities that teach empathy.
    - **Example**: Person picks a card for their group and that card has a description (for example: drug dealer, prostitute, teenage mom). The group then responds to the card. This teaches how it feels to be treated like a stereotype.
    - **Example**: Trade shoes with another person. Have the students walk around and see what it feels like to physically be in someone else's shoes.
    - **Example**: Pick a person or situation where the student would not show empathy (i.e., if someone attacked them or a loved one). Talk about why. After you talked about it, try to find ways that you could display empathy.

## ADVICE TO PARENTS

- Parents could talk to them about different situations to help develop problem-solving skills.
- Explain to kids that everyone has their own story and so everyone is different and has different beliefs.
- Help them understand by volunteering with them for those less fortunate.
- Remind children that every parent is human too. Share your personal stories to help them understand the adult's perspective.
- Help kids understand that no one is perfect.

## ADVICE TO MEDIA

- Create more child-friendly learning shows, such as *Barney* and *Sesame Street*, which focus on being a good friend.

- Define empathy in a child-friendly way, such as a short cartoon between shows.
- Use more empathetic messages in music.
- Teach them to understand why people go through what they go through. Take a stand on what is right.
- Do a "Don't Bully" segment and show them that everyone has problems at times.
- Tell your viewers that they should not take their problems out on other people and instead should talk to people.

# CHAPTER 5:
# THE ABC'S OF PEACE

The C.R.I.M.E. Teens

The ABC'S of Peace were stumbled upon. You see, we were doing presentations for younger kids on Anger Management, Bullying, Conflict-Resolution, and Self Esteem for our Stand Up! Help Out! mentoring program. As we put these words in order, we soon came upon an acronym (A=Anger Management; B=Bullying, C=Conflict Resolution; S=Self-Esteem). These are the topics that we decided to talk to school-age kids about to help stop them from being involved in violence. The reason why we chose these specific aspects to talk about is because these are the areas in which most children who are aged 6-11 wonder and need to know about. All of these can contribute to a violence-free environment in a number of ways. Upon creating presentations, the C.R.I.M.E group decided to create a DVD and workbook to go along with them.

The way that anger management contributes to a violence-free environment is that if people know how to control their anger, they will be less likely to get into fights and arguments. Anger management helps a person become aware of a problem and then you can explore the root situation and get to the bottom of it before it escalates further. So, in teaching about anger management, we think about a couple things. The only way a person is able to be aware of a problem is to first know that he/she is angry because people sometimes do not know this until it is too late. It also helps to know what makes one angry so that he/she knows what type of situations to avoid as well as which people to avoid. Finally, people need to find good ways to deal with angry feelings. How someone manages anger overall creates either a positive or negative outlook on a situation, but if people know themselves and how they react to certain situations, they can contribute to a violence-free environment. These are lessons we taught the younger children.

Bullying is a very good subject matter to know about. C.R.I.M.E. helps people to realize that bullying is one of the biggest causes of violence in schools and it is necessary to prevent it to have violence free-communities. Most children these days think that bullying is just physical, but C.R.I.M.E. helps people to see that bullying can also be verbal or, in other words, what you say to people. When we presented on bullying, we gave advice both to the bullies and the kids who are being bullied. We think it is important to help both in order to stop bullying.

A violence-free life is what most people want in this world. One thing that would help make this want become a reality would be conflict resolution. Conflict Resolution relates very closely to the other subject matters in that conflict resolution teaches people how to solve problems in a good way. It truly causes others to see that having a good solution can fully dissolve a problem. Instead of people turning conflict into fighting or killing, conflict can create a new friendship. The way we handle conflict can greatly determine how our future may play out. We tried to show the kids that they should always step back, think of what decisions will not end in violence, and try their best to not point the blaming finger. We should always try our

best to end conflict in a civilized, respectful and non-violent manner. The conflict resolution part brings out good
ways to solve problems and the basic things we wanted
the kids to take from it were: in order to come up with
resolutions they need to remain calm, cool, and collected
and do their best to disperse problems.

Lastly, Self Esteem is an aspect of the ABC'S that
contributes to a violence-free environment in that if
people feel good about themselves, they will not feel the
need to hurt or talk about others in a negative way. We
should always think about ourselves in the best way. We
should never let what anyone says about us change the
way we feel about ourselves. People with low self-esteem
tend to become violent and angry toward others. When
people think badly about themselves, they are going to try
and get people to feel the same way that they feel. So, we
taught the kids how to keep only the best thoughts about
themselves and to never let people change how they feel
and think about themselves. This way they will not have
to worry about becoming depressed and not living their
lives. What we think about ourselves is critical in leading a
happy and successful life and in preventing violence in our
communities.

## The Training DVD

The DVD that we created for school-aged kids involved us
addressing the same questions that we did in our presentations, which included:
- What is the definition of the subject we are talking
  about?
- What are examples that may have affected their
  lives?
- What are some tips to deal with these topics in a
  healthy way?

We also put in accompanying skits in which we had children act out the different scenarios that we mentioned in our presentations. This way, the viewing audience could actually get a visual. We hope that teachers can use our DVD as a way to start discussing anger management, bullying, conflict resolution, and self-esteem. Copies of this DVD can be obtained by contacting us at CRIMEteens@gmail.com.

## THE WORKBOOK

The workbooks that we created were a more in depth analysis of the four subjects that we covered. In the beginning of the book, we put the story of our mascot Suluhu. Afterwards we got right into the four ABCS of C.R.I.M.E that we discussed. Some of our activities in the book included crossword puzzles, bingo, coloring sheets, etc. At the very end of the workbook, we had our PLEDGE OF PEACE which basically had ten statements that the reader would agree to or would try to uphold in promoting peace. We hoped that the kids would take the workbooks home so that they can work on them with their parents.

## OUR MASCOT: SULUHU THE PEACE DRAGON

The name of our mascot is Suluhu. We chose the name "Suluhu" because we wanted a word that meant peace in a different language—so we found out this is how you say "peace" in Swahili! We also put three heads on our dragon because three heads are better than one and it symbolizes unity. We chose a dragon for our mascot because dragons are very powerful creatures and C.R.I.M.E. is a very powerful group. The reason why we chose the color purple was because purple can represent peace. We wanted to portray a happy dragon, looking forward to a world of peace and love.

## Suluhu's Story

The following is the story of Suluhu that we tell to younger children:

Suluhu is a Chicago dragon who believes in peace over violence. In fact Suluhu means "peace" in Swahili. He's always bouncing and flying with glee. With a heart like a magnet, Suluhu is able to attract those who have never felt compassion. Suluhu is a firm believer in giving respect to receive respect. By putting his three brains together, Suluhu is able to inspire others. Suluhu has the ability to move others with his fiery words. Although he doesn't have feet, Suluhu has the power to put himself in others' shoes. Finally, he is able to whack out CRIME with his mighty tail.

| 111

In 2010, Suluhu's story will be greatly expanded as we will be writing a book of short stories about how Suluhu deals with the ABC'S of Peace; so, be on the look-out for that book to share with your younger children!

## What We Teach

In this section, we are going to present the basic outline and content of our speeches to the younger children. Of course, with every audience, we changed our presentations a little and had different questions to answer and activities to do with the kids. We hope this gives teachers, parents, and other helping adults ideas on how to present these topics to kids.

## ANGER MANAGEMENT
## CREATED PRIMARILY BY DESIREE TELLIS

"Anger will never disappear so long as thoughts of resentment are cherished in the mind. Anger will disappear just as soon as thoughts of resentment are forgotten."

—Siddharta Guatama, Buddha

In discussing Anger Management, we tackled three big questions:
- What is anger management?
- Why do we get angry?
- What are some practical ways in which we can control our anger?

First, we asked the kids about what makes them angry. We got many different answers, including the following:

- What makes me angry is when someone talks about me.
- I get angry when some pulls my hair.
- I get angry when someone takes my stuff.
- I get angry when my little sister messes up my room.
- I get angry when I can't go outside or I can't watch television.

Then, to get them thinking about the topic, we give a scenario and ask the kids to tell what would be the good thing to do and what would be the bad thing to do. The scenario is:

John and Tommy are playing basketball. Tommy accidentally fouls John and John thinks that he did it on purpose.

Here we get a bunch of different responses, but we hope the kids can see ways for John to stay calm, avoid a fight, and talk out the problem with Tommy.

Next, we talk about the importance of being able to

control our anger and reasons why.  Some reasons we give and have gotten from the kids are:

- You won't get suspended from school.
- You won't get detention.
- You won't get in trouble with your parents.
- It will make you a better person.
- You have more friends.
- You'll be more likeable.

To end the presentation, we talk about different ways to handle anger and practice these with the kids. Some examples are:

- Take a deep breath.
- Listen to music.
- Talk to an adult/peer.
- Exercising.
- Writing.
- Punching a pillow.

## BULLYING
### CREATED PRIMARILY BY MONIQUE RATCLIFF & KING SAMI

*"Never be bullied into silence. Never allow yourself to be made a victim. Accept no one's definition of your life, but define yourself."*

—Harvey S. Firestone

First, we ask the kids if they know what a bully is. When we get those answers, we explain what bullying behavior is:

It is someone saying or doing something that makes someone feel hurt, scared, sick, lonely, embarrassed or sad. For example, bullies might hit, kick, or push to hurt someone. Or they may use words to call names, threaten tease, or scare someone. Also, trying to frighten or control someone is bullying behavior. So, a bully might say mean things about someone, grab someone's stuff, make fun of someone, or leave a person out of a group on purpose.

We then set up a skit with the kids in our audience: One student comes up to a group of three kids and comes over and knocks a book out of one of their hands and calls that child "Stupid."

We then ask the audience about what had happened to help them see an example of bullying in everyday life.

After this skit, we ask the kids if they have ever been bullied and if they have ever been a bully. We use empathy with both groups and tell them we are going to help them both.

The kids ask us a lot, "Why are we being bullied?" To answer this, we tell the older kids (fourth & fifth graders):

Another kid may feel unwanted, unloved, or not good about him or herself. Then, he or she may throw angry feelings out on others. Other times, they may just be

looking for attention or trying to make themselves feel
nportant. Also, sometimes, they might just come
family that is angry and shouting all the time
ink this is a normal way to act. Also, some might
ieen bullied before and then when they got big-
iey become a bully.
e explain it to the younger kids (first, second, &
lers) like this:
er kid may be angry for many different reasons
akes it out on others. They also may not know
:o be a good friend and they need adults and
kids in their class to help teach them that.
e end our presentation by going over tips for how
e bullies and what to do if you are a bully.

For: Erika Tello

v to handle run-ins with bullies and to avoid run-
ins with bullies:

| 115

1. Never put on a sad face when a bully is around.
2. Walk away from trouble if you need to.
3. Get an adult to help you if you need to.
4. Try to ignore the bully (don't give the bully a chance).
5. Take a deep breath.
6. Count to ten.
7. Turn insults into compliments.
8. Show you understand what is upsetting a person.
9. Say what you're feeling (I-Statements).
10. Stand tall and be brave.

Tips: for the people who are bullying:
1. It's okay to be mad, but don't take it out on others.
2. Use your words instead of your fists.
3. Treat all living thing with respect.
4. You can't have your own way all the time.
5. Don't sweat the small stuff.
6. Let you anger go in safe ways.
7. CHILL OUT!

## Conflict Resolution

*"It isn't enough to talk about peace, one must believe it. And it isn't enough to believe in it, one must work for it."*

—Eleanor Roosevelt

We start off our presentation by asking the audience, "What is CONFLICT?" Then, we give the following definition.

Conflict is when someone or a group wants something but the other wants something else. It is like people disagreeing, fighting, or arguing over something.

Then, we ask them about what kind of conflicts they deal with. Some of the common ones the kids tell us about are:

- Other kids talking about them or hitting them.
- Their parents not allowing them to go outside because they didn't clean up.
- Their little brothers/sisters doing things and getting away with it.
- Their teachers asking them to do things that they don't want to do.

We then talk about why handling conflict in a peaceful way is so important. These are the important reasons:

- You will maintain friendships.
- You will not get into trouble.
- You will display a mature attitude.
- You will become a well-rounded person in the long run.

We end our presentation by giving tips for conflict resolution. These include:

1) Top No, No's

- When you are in a disagreement with someone there should be no yelling, screaming, kicking, fighting, name calling, or threats.

- There should also be no put downs, or bad words that could hurt someone's feelings.
- Remember to treat everyone the way you would want to be treated.

2) Your Feelings
- When you get mad, go somewhere else to cool off.
- If someone hits you, don't hit back. Just walk away.
- If they keep on doing it, then tell a teacher or an adult.

3) Talking
- Talk one at a time and listen.
- Don't make any blames or bring up secrets. That could make the person even madder.
- Talk using eye contact and use the word "I" to express how you feel.

4) Think!, Think!, Think!
- Put on your thinking cap and brainstorm ways for you and the person to fix the problem.
- Think about the problem.
- Say what you feel and have others do the same.
- Decide on what you all want to do.
- Stick to what you've decided on what to do.
- Then talk again if the problem isn't solved.

## Self-Esteem

*"You must love yourself before you love another. By accepting yourself and fully being what you are, your simple presence can make others happy."*

—Unknown

In talking about self-esteem, we start with a group discussion, asking the kids such questions as:

- What makes you feel good about yourself?
- What do you like about yourself?
- What are some of your talents?

We then tell the kids how great they are and how many wonderful talents are in the room. We tell the kids that even though they are great, sometimes they may not feel good about themselves. We have another talk, asking the kids:

- Are there ever times you are mad at yourself or feel bad about yourself?

After this discussion, we explain self esteem as: It is how you think about yourself. It can be in a negative or positive way. Sometimes, if you lose a game or someone calls you a name, you might feel bad about yourself. But, we want for you all to feel good about yourselves all of the time.

We then give the following situation and at the end, ask the kids what they did wrong or right.

Justin and Case are playing a game of air hockey at Justin's house. Justin always wins when he plays air hockey but he seems really upset about something (hey kids can you predict what happens next?). When the game starts, Case keeps scoring while Justin is missing the blocks. Now that made Justin even madder. Well, Justin then gets really angry.

We have the kids think about what is going to happen this time:

- Should he kick Case out?
- Say he's really bad at the game and tell Case he's
- not going to play anymore?
- Tell Case what's making him mad and keep trying?

We try to get the kids to see that telling people your problems can always relieve stress and it can make you feel better if you are feeling bad about yourself.

We end the presentation by telling them that there are eight good things to do for themselves:

1. Do things that make you feel good like going swimming, making models, doing art, or playing sports.
2. Give yourself a treat every day, like playing with your toys, eating a piece of candy, or taking a hot bath with bubbles.
3. Forgive yourself for what you did a while ago and learn from it so you don't do it again.
4. Do something good for your body, like exercising. You can do it at home by helping with the case of water, running, or doing push-ups—anything that can keep your heart pumping.
5. Do something good for your brain. Playing a checkers/ chess game or even Monopoly keeps you thinking.
6. Find grown-ups you feel cool to talk to because that can make you feel like a better person.
7. When you hear bad comments from others or even in your head, remember the good things and know that your body is yours no matter what shape or size and that there are things about yourself you can't change.
8. Talk to yourself and always tell yourself all about your talents and all the great things in your life. You should give yourself at least three compliments a day.

We always end our presentation with The Pledge of Peace. This is a document created by the C.R.I.M.E group which was basically a promise to uphold the values that were being taught to the children. It discussed maintaining peaceful attitudes and relations with others. The Pledge for Peace was a pledge which meant to get the kids to think in one of two ways:

- I am willing to take the needed steps on this document to be a better person.

OR

- If I am a person who already does these things, I will continue to be this way.

The Pledge of Peace was just a written statement showing the willingness to change, but true change lies within our person.

120 |

## THE PLEDGE OF PEACE

I _____promise that

1. I will not let my anger get the best of me.
2. If I'm mad I will not hit anyone.
3. I will avoid violence at all cost.
4. If I am being bothered I will walk away.
5. I will remember the ABC'S of Peace.
6. I will help others to live a peaceful life.
7. I will consider others' feelings.
8. I will solve problems verbally and not physically.
9. I will keep a peaceful attitude.
10. I will uphold and remember this Pledge of Peace.

Signature _____

# CHAPTER 6:
# LETTERS TO ADULTS

This chapter is a compilation of letters that teens on the South Side of Chicago wrote to parents and adults about what needs to be done in terms of youth violence.

| 121

Dear Parents,

Nowadays violence has become a large issue in our communities. It seems as if you can't go anywhere without something occurring. For example, I heard on the news when a young girl and her brother went to the store around the corner, and on their way they were robbed for their cell phone and the grocery money. I think violence is such a big problem because of the bad economy and problems within families. I think the economy has a lot to do with the violence of today because since a lot of people can't afford things, they choose to steal, kill, or die for things.

Violence has affected my life in many ways, seeing that I grew up around it my entire life. Throughout my life I have seen people be killed, robbed, and sexually abused. There has also been many times I almost got robbed, and safely got away. I don't think parents understand the exact reason children or teens become involved in violence because they always tend to think teens don't really know what's going on. For example, a teen knows that their family is having some tough problems, but the parent tries to hide them. The teen then wants to make the situation better and chooses to sell drugs to lessen some of the money problems. They also seem to never really pay as much attention to their children. I believe children or teens become involved in things such as violence because of peers, wanting to make money, problems at home, and some are just bored and looks forward to trying new things.

Some of this violence can be prevented. For example, a lot of guys like to play sports, so why not have more sport-oriented activities? So, all I'm saying is even though the economy is bad at the moment, gyms could provide teens with something to do. To give young women of today something to do, groups can be formed to help them express themselves, such as poetry. So in conclusion, I recommend people try and help teens with problems and give them opportunities as well as provide them with something to do. So everyone can lend a helping hand to help a teen, helping the world become a better place.

Sincerely,
Derek Matthews, 15
Dunbar High School

Dear Adults,

There are a lot of things adults or just people can tell kids about not getting involved with violence but it's really up to the child to become a part of it or not. One way I think parents can tell their child is to tell them to think about your future and if you are putting yourself in harms way, you might not make it to that basketball player, singer, or doctor you want to be. I also think it's a problem because all the rappers that kids look up to are saying that smoking weed and gang banging is cool. Kids think it's cool to because their idol does it.

I think violence had affected just about everybody's life in many ways. The way violence had affected my life is when I see on the news that people are being shot and killed just standing on the bus stop, and that makes me think about "what if that was me or anybody I knew?" Violence had affected me in a good way too because by me seeing others being affected makes me not want to hang out with friends in places that gives a bigger chance of putting us in harms way and also made me want to do more with my life so when I get older I can help kids to not become involved or get affected by it like I have.

I think there are a lot of reasons adults don't understand why kids get involved with violence. I think the number one reason is adults think that just because when they were our age, their parents didn't allow them to do it so they don't see why parents do now. I'm not saying it's right for parents to; I'm just saying it's not how it used to be when they were growing up and it's a whole new group of parents and also kids. I also think adults don't understand because they are not a child. Just like when adults say we don't understand because we are kids, they don't understand because they are adults. And they also say "I been there and done all your tricks and stuff you haven't even thought of yet" but that's not true because kids don't think the way they used to these days. So, adults need to work to understand how today's kids are different instead of being "know-it-alls."

I think children are involved in violence because their lives are not what they want it to be. They don't feel loved, and they don't have anything else better to do. Also many kids do it to fit in because you have the type of kids who are cool because they sell drugs and smoke weed but I think those are the lames in my eyes. On a positive note, some children aren't even involved in violence and try to remove themselves from it but it comes to them.

My suggestion for preventing youth violence is to first stop the adults who are giving youth the drugs and guns because it has to start somewhere and 90% of the time it's not from the kid. I also think we should have more FREE after school programs for kids until their parent comes to pick them up. I think people can do a lot about youth violence; they just are lazy and don't.

To conclude my paper is I think violence is a problem now because people don't think much of themselves and want to be with the cool crowd which in my eyes is the lame crowd. I think youth violence or any violence can be put to a stop and hopefully President Obama can make change as he said he would.

Sincerely,
Chelbi Hayes, 14
VOISE Academy

Dear All Adults:

Every time I see someone my age dead or hurt because of violence, I just want to cry. Violence is getting worse and worse because of gangs. Gangs get upset if they see other people are better than them. Sometimes, I feel you don't understand why people do what they do. Some think it's no home training or the devil in them, but give them the benefit of the doubt. They have nobody. They are lonely and need people to guide them. YOU! Kids get involved in violence because of lack of care; nobody cares about them so they tend to hurt other people. Other parents need to talk to kids, take them in, and comfort them. Teachers must show that what the kid is doing will hurt them in the long run and show them love. The media should start putting out programs for under privileged youth and help out more and talk about making it. So many kids out there are being killed because of the lack of help from adults.

Sincerely,
Ryan Alexander, 16
Dunbar High School

Dear Parents:

Honestly, to me, I think violence is a problem because adults are not involved. This is one of the reasons why a lot of children are dying and turning their lives over to the streets. Also, because parents don't give their child the attention he or she needs and wants. Violence has affected my life because my mother let violence go on in our house, such as child abuse. My mom and her husband try, but my little brother and I don't let that happen.

Teens and kids are lost to the streets because parents don't give their children enough attention and enough of their time that we need. So, that's why us teens turn to gangs and other family members or peers for the love and support that our parents are not giving us. Adults don't understand that us teens and kids want their attention, love, and support to no matter how old we get. But, we also need our space from parents as well and if our parents do that, maybe we would not turn toward the street for all our wants and needs.

OK, here are some suggestions and ideas I have for preventing violence. I think the media can try to get the point across on ways that parents and teens can better their bonding relationship. So, we, Black people, can live longer and make our world a better place to live, work, and to just be at. Second, I think parents should and could pay more close attention to their children, talk to them more about the rights and wrongs, the do's and don't's. Therefore, they can know who to choose who to hang with and be with. Lastly, the teachers can help students with ways to stay active and out of trouble. They can be positive so the students can be going down the right path. Also, they can help parents understand why it's important for young people to stay active and get involved in extra programs.

Sincerely,
Deangelo Martin, 15
Dunbar High School

Dear Adults,

I think violence is a problem now because people always want to be greedy and disrespectful. When people feel disrespected, they sometimes react in violence because it's all they know and they feel that that's the only way to get rid of the problem. There is a lot of violence over simple things like fights and when one loses, they want to go get guns to kill because they were embarrassed.

Violence has affected my life in many ways because every time you look up, someone has been killed or shot. And it kills me to know that people are getting killed over coats and shoes and that's crazy how kids can get guns and use them for any reason just because they have possessions. I try my best to stay away from violence because I don't wanna get hurt or involved in anything.

I think some adults don't understand why kids get involved in violence because some kids are ashamed or embarrassed to tell what happened or just try to fit in. Some parents may not understand why their children join a gang but it could be just because their child wanted to fit in with their friends or they just thought it was cool. Some kids get involved in violence because they are upset or want revenge on someone and parents wouldn't understand because they don't talk to their children enough.

I think some ways of preventing kids from getting involved with violence is by starting and getting them involved in more after school activities and youth programs that help them or they can help little kids to get them focused on and know what they world is really like. I think some parents should talk with their children more and get involved in their outside lives and find out what's going on with them emotionally just to see what they are feeling.

I am recommending that we, as a family, should all come together and start a "Stop the Violence" Campaign to prevent things from happening. I would also recommend that more after school programs would spread with more sports so kids can become more interested in having fun than putting their life or someone else's life at risk.

Sincerely,
Bernard Robinson, 16
DuSable High School

Dear Adults:

Violence is the main problem in today's society. The main reason why violence is such an issue is because of parents, teachers, and media. If parents are being a positive role model at home and monitoring what their children do, then that would slow the violence down. Many parents allow their children to watch whatever is on the television, they do not realize how powerful the effect has on kids. If parents were more in control then the violence would slow down dramatically.

Violence has affected my life in many different ways. I can recall the time when a fight broke out while I was living in the Ida B. Wells. The result of this fight was the death of my godfather. Seeing things like this tore me up in the inside, but it also made me a better person. It made me want to do better and not become a statistic.

Sometimes adults do not realize how hard peer pressure is. They see it as they have already been there or in that situation and they got through it so their kids can. They don't realize that kids can be persuasive and if you are a weak-minded person, you will fall for anything. Some kids are just afraid of getting hurt so they join the people who they think are going to help them.

Children and teens get involved in violence because they don't have a stable family to go to. They are also afraid of the person running the gangs. Many kids just want to be wanted. Not all children fall under peer pressure because they don't have stable home environments. Most kids that do are trying to portray an image for other people.

I really do not think that youth violence can be stopped or prevented a whole lot. This reason is because violent people have their own mindset. But, if you want to do something about that mindset, a suggestion would be to get the kids involved in positive things. These things can include programs, such as After School Matters, the YMCA, and other social positive activities. This will slow it down.

Parents need to take control of their children. They need to monitor what they do, who they are around, and what they watch. Parents also need to be more involved in their kids' lives. Some parents let the streets and schools raise their children. This is where they go wrong at.

Sincerely,
Jaytonya Peterson, 17
Hyde Park High School

# CHAPTER 7: REFLECTIONS ON THE C.R.I.M.E EXPERIENCE

The C.R.I.M.E. Teens

This chapter is a compilation of interviews conducted with the eight teens that were a part of the C.R.I.M.E. project. In these interviews, the teens talk about their motives for joining the program, their experiences in educating younger children about violence prevention, and their closing messages to adults about this matter.

## INTERVIEW WITH TIARA OUSLEY
*Why did you join this project?*
I joined this project because I wanted to be a part of something very positive and because I want to be a role model someday. I knew that something like this would give me a head start.

*What do you hope this project accomplishes?*
I hope that this project stands out a lot more than the other violence prevention programs because I feel like this one was very unique. I hope that people take this seriously and like it a lot. I think that it deserves a lot of recognition from the hard work and time we've put into it. I also just hope that people love the book and learn many life lessons.

*What was your favorite part of doing the project?*
My favorite part was being around the people I care about and writing the book.

*What was your least favorite?*
There was no least favorite to me; everything just taught me many lessons.

*What do you think the young kids learned from the presentations?*
I think that they learn that their actions also count and although some parents teach their children negative ways on how to deal with violent situations, I think that they learned other ways to deal with hard times.

*Talk about two times you felt that the kids really understood what you were talking about.*

I felt like they really understood what I was talking about when I mentioned ways to deal with anger and how not to retaliate to others in violent ways. They just knew that they can get away with certain things because they are young, but they will use those lessons in the future. When I talked to the kids about violent situations, like domestic violence, they really understood me when I mentioned to talk to their teachers because some of them do look to their teachers for strength.

*Talk about a time you were frustrated when presenting to the kids.*
I wasn't ever frustrated presenting to the kids. It was more like I wished I could tell them something I knew for sure they would follow, like telling them to not act in such violent ways, but sometimes you got to hear things more than once so it can get through your head.

*Did you notice a difference when you talked to kids in different communities or of different races?*
I think the only difference is that the kids did become more compassionate towards others when they were reminded to talk things out and to not get caught up in negativity. That just helps them make friends instead of losing them, because some kids just always argue and fight.

*What was the saddest thing you heard when you talked to the kids about violence?*
The saddest thing I heard was when one child talked about seeing someone gets beat on the streets and vividly described the blood coming down their faces.

*What is your best memory of presenting to the kids?*
My best time was just bonding with the kids I already knew and bonding with some I didn't, it was kind of like being a big sister. Going to a Hispanic neighborhood that day was one of those moments when reality kicked in. That day I felt like a role model and I felt like I had some type of positive influence on them. When I was telling the adorable children ways to cope with and handle violence, I was shocked to hear the experiences they vividly told me. I've experienced many types of violence but I could never retell the moments as well as they did. They spoke on seeing people beat on, killed, shot, domestic violence, and the list just keeps going on. My heart went out to them that very moment. I really wanted to hug all of those children and tell them that everything would be alright. But even I wasn't sure if that would be the case. When I first walked on those streets the neighborhood looked so friendly, but those children stories reminded me that the simplest things can look so innocent but be so bad. Then, on top of it all their school was poor it just shows how good teens like me got it going to a school that can af-

ford decent books. My high school was gigantic and rich compared to theirs. I became very appreciative that minute. I bet that most of those kids looked forward to school as their comfort and strength, to get by the rough days of life. And to be honest I never really cared much about utilizing the skills I was teaching those kids that day, but just hearing their stories made me open minded about using them. I now use those skills and I will only fight if my life is threatened and at times for defense.

*What was it like for you in surveying the community about violence?*
Surveying the Oak Wood Shores community was quite interesting. Female teens were more interested in the surveys rather than the teen boys. The children ages 7-12 were just happy to do them. The children wrote how they would get bullied and how there would be fights in school. They wrote how they could come to their teachers and parents for help. The teens wrote about their experiences with gang affiliation and how it was one of the causes of violence. Some teens felt safer with cops and that more police would help decrease violence in communities. But some felt that the suggestion would have an opposite effect, that they didn't like police. The teens' protection was their fists. Everyone was basically hopeless about any solutions decreasing violence, and they had no clue how to solve violence. All everyone knew was what they went through and that violence is consistently on the rise.

*What is your final message to all kids who might bully or use violence?*
My message to them is everything you say or do will come back to you, so no matter what, always be nice because that is strength. Being mean is a weakness. It's an easy way to behave. So change the negative thoughts you have

because some of those thoughts can become actions. Treat life with respect because that just shows your true character.

*What is your advice for adults working with kids who are trying to help them?*
My advice is to be open-minded and you can always learn from everyone. Lastly, don't let your opinions keep you away from actually considering taking great advice from children.

INTERVIEW WITH DOMONIQUE RATCLIFF
*Why did you join this project?*
The reason I joined this project was because I wanted to learn new things and how to help kids during life.

*What do you hope this project accomplishes?*
I hope this project accomplishes us doing presentations and helping kids accomplish more things—and helping more.

| 135

*So what was your favorite part of doing this project?*
My favorite part was presenting to the kids.

*What was your least favorite part?*
I don't have a least favorite part.

*Ok. What do you think the younger kids learned from the presentation?*
I think they learned how to prevent violence and what to do if they are being bullied.

*Talk about two times that the kids really understood what you were talking about.*
When we did a presentation and I was talking about put-

ting yourself in someone else's shoes and another one, when I was talking to kids about it being ok to stand up for yourself but you have to do it in a good way not a bad way.

*Talk about a time you were frustrated with presenting to the kids.*
One time I was frustrated was when we were trying to present and they were asking lots of questions.

*Did you notice a difference in answers when you talked to kids from different communities or kids of different races?*
I noticed a difference in different communities because some have more quiet kids and ask only one or two questions and some kids in other communities asked more questions because they could understand more.

136 |

*What was the saddest thing you heard when you talked to the kids about violence?*
The saddest thing was one kid said he got bullied everyday and it makes him want to do bad things like bully someone else.

*What is your best memory when presenting to the kids?*
My best memory presenting to the kids is when I do my part, conflict resolution.

*What is your final message to all kids who might bully or use violence?*
My final message to all the kids who may bully or use violence is, always tell an adult, don't be scared to talk about your feelings.

*What is your advice for adults working with kids who are trying to help them?*
My advice for adults working with kids is always work

with the kids and listen to what they have to say because it might help you by listening to them to be a better parent.

## Interview with Brandon Copeland

*Why did you join this project?*
The reason that I joined this project was because I wanted to help younger children out.

*What do you hope this project accomplishes?*
To show children and adults right from wrong.

*So what was your favorite part of doing this project?*
To go out to the schools and hear other people's problems. That was also my favorite thing.

*What was your least favorite part?*
Nothing really.

*What do you think the younger kids learned from the presentation?*
They learned that there are different types of bullying and how to have good self-esteem.

*Talk about two times that the kids really understood what you were talking about.*
When I discussed self-esteem and had them write on a card the best things that they can do and another time was when Monique was doing bullying and showed them a scenario.

*Talk about a time you were frustrated with presenting to the kids.*
When the kids would not listen.

*Did you notice a difference in answers when you talked to kids from different communities or kids of different races?*
They all seemed the same.

*What is your best memory when presenting to the kids?*
When a little boy kept saying "cool."

*What was your least favorite memory?*
When a kid told us he kept seeing someone get beat up.

*What is your final message to all kids who might bully or use violence?*
What goes around, comes around.

*What is your advice for adults working with kids who are trying to help them?*
It takes time and patience.

## INTERVIEW WITH DESIREE TELLIS
*Why did you join this project?*
I joined because it sounded interesting and I would get service learning hours. I also felt like kids don't know enough about violence and need to get the point of it.

*What do you hope this project accomplishes?*
Teaches kids that violence isn't a way of life and that they use the four things that we told them about if they truly want a better life.

*So what was your favorite part of doing this project?*
I enjoyed speaking and educating the children. It also helped me with my public speaking skills.

*What was your least favorite part?*
There was a lot of writing and it was very time consuming.

*What do you think the younger kids learned from the pre-sentation?*
There are different ways to control anger and it also helped bullies to fix their problems in a peaceful way; conflict resolution and how to help them feel better about themselves.

*Talk about two times that the kids really understood what you were talking about.*
The first time, was when we went to LaGrange, they participated and really understood what we were saying.

*Talk about a time you were frustrated with presenting to the kids.*
At one school they continued to play and laugh and not all kids wanted to sit. It was very frustrating and out of hand.

*Did you notice a difference in answers when you talked to kids from different communities or kids of different races?*
There was a huge difference. African American and Hispanic children saw a lot of kids fight or getting hit in the head with a bottle but in other neighborhoods with Caucasians, a lot of the kids said that their sister took their game or something along those lines. The situations weren't as serious.

*What was the saddest thing you heard when you talked to the kids about violence?*
The fact that the children saw a man get hit with a glass bottle. It's sad for young kids to see that.

*What is your best memory when presenting to the kids?*
When one little boy kept saying "this is so cool." All the kids wanted to participate.

*What is your final message to all kids who might bully or use violence?*
My final message is: think about the fact that they are kids now and parents will discipline them. But when they get older, the consequences will be different and they could go to jail and that would ruin their future.

*What is your advice for adults working with kids who are trying to help them?*
My advice is to try and put yourself in the child's shoes. Try to act like they understand. Your perspective may be different and try to act like you understand because some kids may feel that they have to do this.

### Interview with Monique Ratcliff
*Why did you join this project?*
When I first heard about the project, it was interesting so I felt like I had a voice that needed to be heard.

*What do you hope this project accomplishes?*
I hope the kids will get a good understanding about what we're teaching them and they will use it in everyday life.

*So what was your favorite part of doing this project?*
Going to different schools and communities and teaching the kids about the various topics.

*What was your least favorite part?*
I did not have a least favorite part.

*What do you think the younger kids learned from the presentation?*
I think they learned that bullies are not always right and that they can go to adults and not put themselves in danger.

*Talk about two times that the kids really understood what you were talking about.*
When, we went to a school and I was telling them things that bullies do, who are bullies and what bullies can do.

*Talk about a time you were frustrated with presenting to the kids.*
One time the kids were asking a lot of questions, which is good, but there were a lot of questions.

*Did you notice a difference in answers when you talked to kids from different communities or kids of different races?*
No.

*What was the saddest thing you heard when you talked to the kids about violence?*
 One little boy said he got picked on everyday and got hit in the face and tripped.

| 141

*What is your best memory when presenting to the kids?*
One of my best memories presenting was when we passed out stress balls and the books.

*What is your final message to all kids who might bully or use violence?*
To keep your head up and don't let the anger take you over. Talk to someone and don't be scared.

*What is your advice to adults working with kids and trying to help them?*
To listen to what the kids have to say. Don't judge them just hear where their coming from.

## Interview with Aaron Shannon

*Why did you join this project?*
I thought it would be pretty cool to say that I helped create a book. Not many people can say they've done that.

*What do you hope this project accomplishes?*
I hope it can turn kids away from the harsh realities that they may live in and try and motivate them and know that they don't always have to live this way and that they can change.

*What was your favorite part of doing this project?*
I liked the whole project.

*What was your least favorite part?*
Waking up early on Saturdays.

*What do you think the younger kids learned from the presentation?*
I think they learned what empathy was and how to self-motivate.

*Talk about two times that the kids really understood what you were talking about.*
I did two presentations and the first time we talked about bullying and they looked like they understood everything we talked about and the other time was self-esteem. They knew how to raise their self-esteem on their own.

*Talk about a time you were frustrated with presenting to the kids.*
The children were more interested in what their friend was talking about and not us; it was frustrating.

*Did you notice a difference in answers when you talked to kids from different communities or kids of different races?*
Not really, they all responded the same.

*What was the saddest thing you heard when you talked to the kids about violence?*
Most of the children were good kids but the saddest was issues between siblings. It was depressing.

*What is your best memory when presenting to the kids?*
All the kids walking away excited about learning about what we just taught them. I like knowing we talked to kids about something they know about and they can apply it to their everyday life.

*What is your final message to all kids who might bully or use violence?*
There are better ways to express yourself then fighting or making someone else's life miserable.

| 143

*What is your advice for adults working with kids to try and help them?*
Always put yourself in their situation, show they under-stand and don't completely ignore what the child is saying because if you were in their shoes you'd want the same thing.

### Interview with Daria Siler
*Why did you join this project?*
I wanted to teach kids about things that I yearned to learn but was never taught.

*What do you hope this project accomplishes?*
I hope CRIME can create awareness about all those who

don't know about violence and help them to learn new ways to approach and handle violence.

*So what was your favorite part of doing this project?*
Seeing the smiles on the kid's faces after we talked to them about violence.

*What was your least favorite part?*
Certain kids are energetic and they were ready to go home and were out of control.

*What do you think the younger kids learned from the presentation?*
I think they learned that there are better ways to deal with violence. They don't always have to retaliate.

*Talk about two times that the kids really understood what you were talking about.*
One time was when a lot of kids raised their hands to ask questions and the second was when kids were curious and asked us questions that we didn't even discuss amongst each other.

*Talk about a time you were frustrated with presenting to the kids.*
There was one time when one little boy kept saying things that were irrelevant to what we were talking about and he could not sit still.

*Did you notice a difference in answers when you talked to kids from different communities or kids of different races?*
No, they were all the same. They had distinct answers to what we were saying. The all had something to say.

*What was the saddest thing you heard when you talked to the kids about violence?*

A little boy said he and his sister didn't get along and she was always bullying him.

*What is your best memory when presenting to the kids?*
A group of kids did a skit and they were energetic and cooperative.

*What is your final message to all kids who might bully or use violence?*
Violence affects more than one person and you should think about it before you do it.

*What is your advice for adults who are working with kids to try and help them?*
I think that adults should be patient and always ask them how they feel about a situation. Because sometimes asking questions can make someone feel better.

## INTERVIEW WITH KING SAMI

*Why did you join this project?*
I joined because of the influence of my mentor and supervisor Jeff and because of the other members of CRIME.

*What do you hope this project accomplishes?*
Hopefully it will inform kids about positive ways to conquer violence and use the tips CRIME has to fight violence.

*So what was your favorite part of doing this project?*
I enjoyed presenting to the kids. Kids are curious and want to learn about violence and ways to vent. I am sure they experience violence everyday whether it be on TV or at home.

*What was your least favorite part?*
I didn't have a least favorite experience, I learned from them all.

*What do you think the younger kids learned from the presentation?*
They learned about Saluhu the Peace Dragon and they were into empathy. It was one of the big ideas. Put yourself in other people's shoes. Most people don't do that and judge. The kids learned to stop and think before they made hasty choices or criticizes one another.

*Talk about two times that the kids really understood what you were talking about.*
When we did the Pledge for Peace they took everything in from the presentation and they pledged to use CRIME instead of using violence.

*Talk about a time you were frustrated with presenting to the kids.*
You always get frustrated when kids are talking and won't settle down.

*Did you notice a difference in answers when you talked to kids from different communities or kids of different races?*
No, kids are going to be kids.

*What was the saddest thing you heard when you talked to the kids about violence?*
We asked the kids have they ever experienced violence and a girl said her brother hit her in the eye. It was very mean, that's how I felt it was sad.

*What is your best memory when presenting to the kids?*
One guy was really into the presentation. He kept saying "cool, cool."

*What is your final message to all kids who might bully or use violence?*
Bullying is a stepping stone to other more violent activi-

ties, which may be more serious than bullying. Before you bully or use violence you should sit down and think about the consequences and actions of your decisions.

*What is your advice for adults who are working with kids to try and help them?*
Adults really need to close their mouth because they tend to always voice their opinion. Sometimes their opinion isn't needed when kids just need to be heard. They need to use the 'E' in CRIME, Empathy.

WE CANNOT ALWAYS BUILD THE FUTURE FOR OUR YOUTH,
BUT WE CAN BUILD THE YOUTH FOR OUR FUTURE

— FRANKLIN D. ROOSEVELT

# CHAPTER 8: THE DYNAMIC PROCESS OF ADOLESCENT IDENTITY: WHAT I LEARNED FROM THE YOUTH

RACHEL KIBBLESMITH, MSW CANDIDATE

Over the last year I worked with project C.R.I.M.E. as an adult mentor and a presentation coordinator. The primary duties I had were to work with our adolescents on developing their workbooks, personal narratives, and traveling with them to their presentations. When I was initially approached about C.R.I.M.E., I was unsure of what to expect. As a Master's student at Loyola University Chicago's School of Social Work, I did not have experience with an adolescent population. I had reservations about how we would be able to work with our high school group to complete a project that required autonomy, motivation, creativity, and commitment.

When project C.R.I.M.E. began, I met a group of enthusiastic and motivated teens. Each youth had joined the group for a different reason: some were excited to put their work on a resume, some were interested in working with children, and some wanted to get their writing published. What every single adolescent did have in common however was that each had a personal and powerful experience with family or community violence and was passionate about finding a way to change it.

The first piece of the project was to discuss with

the students how exactly they would want to spread their message of violence prevention. This was one of the most beneficial pieces of the project, due to the fact that it allowed me to assess how excited each student was about C.R.I.M.E. What I found was that many of the students wanted to spread the message of peace and violence prevention to young children. They also were adamant that they wanted their voices heard by adults who would have power and resources to help them. The fundamental message that I was given when talking with the teens was that they were eager to advocate for safer neighborhoods, schools, and homes.

Tapping into passion is one of the most genuine and powerful ways to engage youth. In my conversations with our teens, many felt that adults did not care about their struggles and that they did not have time to sit and listen to ideas that youth presented. All of our students were passionate about creating a successful future and are doing so by utilizing after school programs, staying away from negative peer influences, and focusing on their academic work.

What I found is that when given an empathic and expressive space, our youth were able to blossom and verbalize exactly what they have experienced, and precisely how they want to change areas in their lives in order to attain their goals. As adults, our role is critical in the sense that we have to allow the space for youth to discuss their goals and assess the best way to harness their passion in a purposeful and meaningful way. One of the ways that we worked with youth to achieve this was by actively listening to their interests to evaluate the best method to engage them. In order to connect with our youth, we had to hear and understand from them what their unique learning styles and talents were.

Learning to understand the unique competencies

of our adolescents was one of the most vital lessons I
learned from our youth. This is an area that I still believe
can be explored by adults. As a group, our adolescents
presented a multitude of different experiences, adaptive
skills, strengths, and emotional literacy. C.R.I.M.E. is unique
due to the fact that it offered adolescents a chance to
utilize their individual strengths, while also being men-
tored on how to increase confidence and competence in
other areas. Our most powerful writers were excited to
assist with literary pieces, while our extroverted students
enjoyed presenting to audiences. Adolescents with artistic
abilities were able to create a mascot, and those interested in business brainstormed and conceptualized mar-
keting materials. Ultimately, each adolescent was given an
opportunity to use his or her unique competence to allow
C.R.I.M.E. to flourish as a cohesive strength based process
and holistic learning experience.

     Understanding youth thinking styles and allowing | 151
them to find their passion was instrumental in the success
of our project. I believe that adults can access a higher
level of engagement in youth by taking additional time
to support them in an active learning process in which
adults are truly interested in utilizing youth's strengths.
Additionally, by providing positive feedback and mentorship
in areas where youth felt they had deficits, C.R.I.M.E. gave
our teens the chance to feel successful performing tasks
that they had never attempted.  By allowing adolescents
to become the leaders in their learning process, they were
inspired to more fully commit to C.R.I.M.E.

     Another area that I had to deeply consider when
working with an adolescent population is their developmental stage. Adolescence is often viewed as a tumultuous
time in an individuals' life. Youth are often perceived as
emotional, confused, and easily subjected to peer pressure.
Adolescents may also exhibit an increase in problematic

behaviors, in both home and school environments. This is often due to flirtation with autonomy, and experimentation with expanding their childhood boundaries. While some adults might view this as a frustrating process that adolescents will eventually "grow out of," this viewpoint can be detrimental to an adolescent's positive identity development.

Adolescence is not just a phase of maturation. It is a dynamic and vital step toward achieving an adult identity. Adults can view adolescent development as a vibrant and vital identification process. By becoming optimistic about teens and accessing the excitement that adolescence can provide, adults can more thoroughly understand the emotional and psychological adolescent experience. This is also a period when critical interventions can be put into place for at risk adolescents who may have never received help. Adults can reach out to children who are in the process of changing and forming their identities and assist them in accessing information and resources that they may have otherwise never received. Despite the stereotypes that can plague adolescents, there are many who are craving adult respect and positive attention. I learned that adults could work with youth on their identification process to further understand the benefits of this stage in the life cycle. By using a strength-based approach to adolescent development, I believe that it has helped our adolescents grow immensely in their emotional maturation, rationality, and overall positive identity.

Ultimately, what adults can learn from C.R.I.M.E. is to set aside time to spend delving deeper into youth's needs. From conversations I have had with our teens, surveys we distributed to other youth, and advice that our group has given adults, it is clear that the single most important message that youth have relayed is that they need adults to hear their voice. This is of particular importance when working with adolescents from marginalized and disenfranchised communities. Too often their needs have been ignored. It has been too long that their voices have been tuned out.

When you read the personal experiences of our youth, it becomes clear that there have been too many times when their lives have been subjected to uncertainty, violence, and danger. And while these experiences are personal to our youth, the overall climate of violence, lack of resources, and neglect is rampant and resonates with the broader society. Project C.R.I.M.E. has been unique due to the fact that it has sought out to find youth leaders in unlikely places. I can honestly say that I have witnessed each and every one of our adolescents step up and become a leader, and a passionate agent for social change. As an adult community, we need to access these youth leaders and to provide them with the resources and power to make positive change. This is not something that should happen. This is something that must occur.

## The Battle to End Destructive Mentalities
### Tiara Ousley

Bullets are popped and bodies are shattered
A hopeless era that no one can stop
All because we don't have the power
So religions are looked to, to cope with the ordeal
Pain is a horrible feeling that we wish wasn't real
So what can we do to better our world?
Can we fight the evil temptation in ourselves
To avoid the destruction of our people and land?
I don't think so, unless we give it a try
People are tired of the violence in this world
So, what can we do in order to win?
To win these battles and to defeat this war
We have to dig into the roots of our communities
To change the mentalities of our people
And to end this petty racism, prejudice, and horrible lies
Someone's gotta be our savior, someone's gotta be brave
So we gotta stand up and help out in order to be saved

We gotta stick together in order to not fall apart
We can't wait til the last minute and we can't let time be
the enemy
So we gotta start now and make time our friend

So let's not give up
Instead, let's make sure destructive mentalities come to an
end.

PEACE IS NOT SOMETHING YOU WISH FOR, IT'S SOMETHING
YOU MAKE, SOMETHING YOU DO, SOMETHING YOU ARE, AND
SOMETHING YOU GIVE AWAY.

—ROBERT FULGHUM

# CHAPTER 9: WHERE DO WE GO FROM HERE?

KING SAMI AND DESIREE TELLIS

Where do we go from here? Have we just wasted our time and energy by publishing another anti-violence book that will collect dust? Or, have we written a book that will inspire others to develop a world of compassion, respect, inspiration, motivation, and empathy? Our book can only bite off a piece of the problem called violence, so now it is time for individuals, schools, businesses, and the government to take action.

In my world literature class, we finished reading the novel Paradise of the Blind; reading the novel, I've retained information about the Vietnamese culture. They have an outstanding way of caring for strangers and family, yet in our nation, money drives people's ambitions. It is insane how corporations spend millions advertising their products for a boost in profit, but our violence prevention group had to compete with numerous other groups for just $5000. How come we cannot profit from mass media also? How come anti-violence efforts are not funded as much as materialistic wants? We as a nation have let violence go on for too long. How many innocent lives must others take? How many teens have to die? How many children have to be frightened to walk outside of their home?

Let's start by thinking about how to end violence in schools. To our peers—our brothers and sisters—you need to let words just be exactly what they are—letters in the alphabet—when they have an inappropriate meaning. Be bigger than the words that are flung at you. Teachers have to realize that they have a bigger role than just teaching students. A teacher-student relationship can minimize violence within classrooms. Encouraging students to participate in class or after school extracurricular activities allow students to benefit from having fun rather than spending time being idle.

Also, schools are kind of one-sided in supporting athletic teams instead of more clubs. There must be more programs to fill the void for others that do not play sports. One perfect example is After School Matters. To have fun in an informative program that interests you may help you pick your future career. ASM includes a stipend as a way to get the attention of all those individuals that need to be pushed and those that need a job to just help their family survive. Although ASM is an awesome program that prevents violence, it is being cut. In actuality, it needs to be expanded and diversified.

Beyond After School Matters, our communities need to offer more programs for the unemployed (especially, high school drop-outs and people with GEDs). Programs should help these individuals seek more education. For example, programs can help them get into trade schools and junior colleges as well as help them find jobs and write resumes. These programs will decrease the amount of violent deaths and robberies because the individuals will be able to be productive members of society and find safe and legal ways to make money.

In our mission to prevent some of the violence that goes on in this community, the entire media and music industry need to send more positive messages. Music expresses an artist's creativity, yet music needs to be toned down from the message of killing and violence. Artists need to realize how some of the filthy lyrics that they use just add to the cycle of decadence within this world. Some make kids think that calling women degrading names and treating them so low is okay. They provoke children, teenagers, and even some adults to use their tongues as weapons. Children need to be taught to respect others— not threaten or degrade others. Artists should serve as role models and not problem makers, but sadly many are not conscious to all of the ways their music affects people negatively. We are asking the role models in the music industry to start singing about positive things, like graduating from college, doing a career they love, or overcoming major hurdles.

Next, we want to address the government. Our government is constantly talking about "homeland security," but what about security in warzones on the streets of America? The government's unbalanced budget funds the military (usually without question) taking a huge piece out of the budget. How come the government thinks war will solve any problem? War is brought upon another country because of greed and revenge. War has solved nothing in the past but creates more tension rather than solving the problem at hand. Why is the government neglecting the home land when there has been an ongoing war in the streets with individuals dying every day? Why aren't programs that benefit the decrease in violence funded as much as a new weapons to advance the technology of the military? We need programs that stop the growing population of gangs and programs the help convicts get back on their feet. The government needs to look at the bigger picture at hand: Why is it ok for the military to fight another country while gangs have been fighting one another for decades yet that is considered wrong? Just like we have asked our parents and teachers, government officials, please lead by example! If you do not want the teens on the south side of Chicago killing each other over beef, do not start and continue wars.

If we do not act now on the violence problem, killing someone will become a natural way for solving problems with others. In fact, looking at the wars that go on throughout the world and in the streets of the U.S., it appears this may already be the case. This world continues to become desensitized and accept murder as a part of everyday life. However, we need for everyone to see that killing or hurting anyone (including our enemies) is not acceptable. No one has the right to take someone else's life. When the urge comes, we need to have different options available to prevent others from using any forms of violence.

We, as humans, need to remember that stopping the violence starts with us. Not us as a nation, not us as a community, not us as a family, but as one person. We all are our own person and we make our own decisions. If the whole nation attempts to stop violence, does it really matter? No, it does not because one bad apple spoils the bunch. So, work on you as an individual and then work your way into the group. "Know yourself first, change the world second" is the way it goes, but go beyond that and, "Change yourself first, Change the world second."

# AFTERWORD

Jeffrey J. Bulanda, Ph.D.

Throughout the year of 2009, the teens of the C.R.I.M.E. project critically examined the problem of violence and how to replace aggression with compassion, respect, inspiration, motivation and empathy. As this book comes to a close, I want to highlight some of the key themes and findings that emerged in writing this book, in our group discussions, and in consulting with youth outside of our program.

*Theme #1: Violence is rampant and deeply impacts the youth who are victims, witnesses and sometimes perpetrators.*

When asked to write personal narratives about a time that violence impacted their lives, most of the teens had a number of experiences from which to choose; certainly, we could have filled this entire book with vignettes of times that the eight C.R.I.M.E. teens had witnessed or experienced violence between the fights at school, domestic violence at home, bullying, gossiping, and gang activity in the community. Our eight teens are not anomalies. The 40 teens, who took part in the survey, also reported that violence was a frequent occurrence in their homes, schools, and neighborhoods. Perhaps, most concerning is how complacent many of the teens were in reporting their experiences. The frequency of violence has desensitized them and many do not realize that this is not how life should or could be lived. They live in a dangerous zone and have difficulty imagining life any other way. Indeed, even after the "jumping" incident at our after school program that was described in the first chapter, some of the teens were very matter of fact about the incident and did not understand why we spent two days processing the event; many of them had witnessed firsthand or been a part of such acts on multiple occasions previously and so did not see it as a "big deal" (as one student said).

This theme has implications on a number of levels. First, the significance of violence in inner city communities cannot be minimized or ignored any further. King and Desiree question why the government is spending millions and millions to try to keep peace in other countries, but millions of youth are living in inner city war zones right now in the United States. The other key implication is a recognition of the impact of ongoing violence on the development of youth. Social services are necessary to help youth cope with living in such war zones to minimize the impact of this ongoing trauma. Too few of these youth have access to the counselors and social workers they desperately need. This must be a cornerstone in intervening in this problem; we, as adults, cannot become complacent and just accept that the kids "get used to" the ongoing violence and then expect them to succeed without the necessary support. They certainly will adapt to such conditions, but when that happens, it usually means they turn to embracing the violence as a means of self-preservation.

*Theme #2: Teens challenge the popular stereotype of apathy; many exhibit a level of concern for safety in their communities and are willing to take action if opportunities are provided.*

The second key theme throughout this book is the teens' level of concern and desire for a peaceful world. Certainly, in my years of working with the kids labeled as being "severely emotionally disturbed," "antisocial", and/or "gangbangers," I have found constructive motives in every one of them. Each could identify at least a part of themselves that was seeking to have close relationships and not have worry about being killed when they go out on the streets. So, that is why I am constantly "on my soapbox" that we need to focus on EMPOWERING youth rather than CONTROLLING them into compliance. We need to give them experiences of being cared about and of caring for others. Perhaps, most importantly, we need to give them opportunities to feel empowered in coping with the trauma that has made them feel powerless. Consider our teen, Daria Siler. In her personal narrative, she talked about the pain and struggles of living in a household with domestic violence. This project has given her the opportunity to feel empowered to hopefully make a difference in another family's life. She now realizes how parents should treat each other and how they should care for their children; this is why her plea to stop to physical punishment is so powerful. The implications here are that living in violence can leave a child feeling empty and powerless and, then, they may take control in negative ways (i.e., joining a gang). We need to actively find ways for youth to feel powerful, to see they can trust others, and to feel in control of their minds. In summary, teens are not self-centered and apathetic as they are often portrayed; rather, many are actively taking opportunities to feel connected to their community and to feel they are making a difference. The unfortunate thing is that such opportunities are sparse.

*Theme #3: Not only are teens willing to take action, they demonstrate that they have abilities and insights that are helpful toward the fight against violence.*

As a school social worker in an alternative school for youth with emotional disturbances, I am in a frequent battle to have the youth be involved in important decision-making that impacts them. For example, we have a daily social skills curriculum for the youth. There was a committee of teachers and administrators designated to plan the social skills curriculum; I questioned my social work supervisor about why there were not any students on the committee since social skills is supposed to benefit them. She came back to me a couple weeks later and said that the head administrator said "There will be no students on the committee at this time" with no explanation given. The assumption underlying this adultcentric decision is that youth could not possibly know what is best for them and they would just be a hindrance to the adult decision-making.

164 |

Certainly, I entered the C.R.I.M.E. project feeling that youth are highly competent and capable (my core paradigm in working with all youth). However, I must say that Monique, Domonique, Tiara, Brandon, King, Desiree, Daria, and Aaron even surpassed my high expectations of them. My response consistently when they turned in a writing assignment was "No one is going to believe a teenager wrote this!" That said, I want to highlight here that while adults did help mentor the teens in writing and helped edit this book, the youth chapters were written completely by the teens of C.R.I.M.E. and then integrated by the adult and teen editors. So, the lesson here is that youth can be highly insightful, intuitive, and capable in addressing the problem of violence.

The fourth chapter analyzing the results of the survey exemplifies how capable the youth are. The youth were given a quick briefing on "qualitative data analysis"—basically, told to put responses that were similar into groups and then name those groups. They picked up on this process with very limited direction from the adults. Aaron Shannon was able to almost replicate the categories of violence described in Tolan (2000), a foremost expert on violence prevention. Aaron's categories of "domestic violence," "street/gang violence," and "general violence" greatly overlap Tolan's categories of "interpersonal," "predatory," and "situational violence." Aaron was able to do this without ever reading articles or books from the "experts" on violence prevention. I use this as evidence that youth are underutilized in decision-making, whether they be decisions made at home, how to go about researching and understanding relevant topics, or in designing and evaluating programs/curriculums.

*Theme #4: There is a fine line between the youth who* | 165
*"turn to the street" and the "resilient" youth who turn to a*
*positive outlet.*

  In the literature on violent youth, different trajectories along with risk and protective factors have been identified (see research by Loeber & Stouthamer-Loeber; USDHHS, 2001). Certainly, the consensus is that there are no set ingredients that lead to an individual with antisocial characteristics versus an individual who overcomes the odds and is resilient. What is clear is that there is a fine line between the youth who will become "gangbangers" and those who will become productive citizens. Even in discussions with the youth of C.R.I.M.E., several talked about how they flirted with the street life—by hanging out with gang members and even being tempted by the money that can be earned in drug sales. However, various influences turned them around to become social activists against violence.

Thus, resources and interventions must be instituted with this in mind. Youth are not born to be antisocial. Just as many are always on the cusp of being negatively influenced by peers, many more are on the cusp of excelling in school and becoming role models to younger children. We must be proactive in reaching out to all youth. Often the youth that are "maintaining" (i.e., passing in school with C's or D's, no real behavioral problems, etc.) are assumed to be doing all right and then are ignored as the attention and interventions are directed to the children who are actively acting out. Communities, schools, and parents need to ensure they are piling on the protective factors for those youth "maintaining" because at some point, this minimal level of self-determination could dip and they may take a negative track. Furthermore, those students who excel need to continue to be given opportunities that will challenge, motivate, and empower them. Activities in the classroom that offer empowerment, decision-making at home, encouragement and interest from parents, the availability of mentors and counselors, and opportunities for employment and community service are some examples of how we can be more deliberate in assisting those youth teetering on this fine line.

*Theme #5: We have created a society that craves both verbal and nonverbal violence.*

The C.R.I.M.E. group frequently discussed how the media either embraces or disowns our principles and we discovered numerous examples of how our country seeks out negativity, conflict, gossiping, and fighting. For instance, one can stop by www.perezhilton.com at any time and see how Perez Hilton exploits the mishaps and suffering of celebrities. Rather than showing empathy and compassion for celebrities who are battling addiction or mental illness, he gossips about and makes a mockery of them. He has no regard for how his gossiping or portrayal will impact them or their families, including their young children. Furthermore, if you look at the advertisements for any reality show (i.e., I Love New York, Real World, Jersey Shore), the fighting between the participants is always highlighted to lure in viewers. Even our nightly news is drawn to focusing on the most negative occurrences in the world; acts of harm dominate the news significantly more than acts of altruism. Beyond television, music and video games are also often fixated on negative images. As youth grow up bombarded by conflict, greed, and gossip through music, video games and TV, they lose touch with their innate capacity for compassion, respect, and empathy.

The implications for this theme are reiterated by our teens in the "advice to media" sections in Chapter Five. Children and teens need to be submerged in stories of inspiration and altruism and see that humans are most fulfilled by connecting with others—not demeaning or attacking them. We ask that the media outlets realize they have a responsibility to our youth and our country. Putting out these negative shows/music/video games/blogs have negative consequences that have spiraled out of control in ways ranging from street violence (i.e. the influence of video games like Grand Theft Auto) to cyberbullying (the influence of Perez Hilton, TMZ, etc.). Profiting at the expense of others is not only unethical, but also inhumane. Since there seems to be no end in sight for exploitive media, parents must take action by monitoring what their children are exposed to and being deliberate in ensuring they are developing their capacities for compassion, respect, inspiration, motivation, and empathy.

*Theme #6: Teens want adult involvement from parents, teachers, and mentors.*

In Chapter Eight, Deangelo Martin writes,

> Honestly, to me, I think violence is a problem because adults are not involved...Teens and kids are lost to the streets because parents don't give their children enough attention and enough of their time that we need...Adults don't understand that us teens and kids want their attention, love, and support to no matter how old we get.

This quote exemplifies a theme that comes up throughout this book and that came up in many of our discussions as a violence prevention group. Teens are typically portrayed as being focused primarily on their peer group with little interest in spending time with their parents or other adults. Adolescence is a time of separation and identity development; however, this is a critical period of insecurity and ambivalence that needs to be supported by adults. Therefore, adults need to ensure they are proactive in providing the "attention, love, and support" for teens—even if the teens are initially resistant. Parents need to ensure they are designating "quality time" with their teens; this may mean they give their teens some control in how and when the time is spent together. Teachers need to be proactive in building relationships with their students by getting to them as people and not just as students. Adult mentors need to step up and reach out to youth; this can be done informally by connecting with a nephew or friend's child or formally by joining a mentoring program, such as Big Brothers/Big Sisters.

### Closing and Moving Forward

In closing, we, the collective C.R.I.M.E. group, would like to thank you, the reader, for supporting our efforts. We hope that we have given some "food for thought" and that you begin to contemplate your interactions with the youth in your life in a different way. We are excited that C.R.I.M.E. will continue to fight violence throughout 2010 as our grant has been renewed by the Illinois Violence Prevention Authority. In the next year, we plan to expand our C.R.I.M.E. presentations to junior high students and address that group's unique needs. We also will write a second book. This will be a children's book with short stories about Su-luhu, the Peace Dragon; so, keep an eye out for that in late 2010!

May peace be with you!

THE ONLY PEOPLE WITH WHOM YOU SHOULD TRY TO GET
EVEN ARE THOSE WHO HAVE HELPED YOU.

—JOHN E. SOUTHARD

# BIOS

Jeffrey Bulanda completed his masters and doctoral work at Loyola University Chicago School of Social Work. He has been the Program Director for the Empowering Counseling Program since its inception in Summer 2006. He is committed to issues of social justice and is advancing this agenda through participatory research. Additionally, he is committed to providing and researching effective social work services for disadvantaged youth and families and providing a quality education for social work students.

Rachel Kibblesmith is an M.S.W student at Loyola University Chicago's School of Social Work. She is specializing in School Social Work and has focused on Children and Family Services. Rachel has worked in schools with children and families in Chicago's south side as a counselor and program facilitator and evaluator, and in LaGrange Park IL as a school social work intern. Rachel enjoys working with children, specifically populations of children and families who harbor a multitude of unmet and challenging needs, and hopes to continue to work with children and education upon Graduating from her Master's in Social Work Program in May, 2010.

My name is Brandon Copeland. I grew up in suburbs of Florida and did not have too many friends due to my color. To get the lack of friends off my mind, I grew up doing art. I stayed in grammar school in Florida until first grade. After my grandmother had a stroke, I moved to Chicago to live with my mom and I stayed here for eight years so now I still have art as one as my greatest talents. I joined this wonderful group called C.R.I.M.E. to help younger children solve their problem. I'm the artist for the group, so art is still very important to me.

My name is Tiara Ousley. I'm sixteen years old, and I go to Curie High School. I have dreams of becoming a big time actress and author. I love to run, sing, dance, skate, meet new people, and hang with family. Someday I want to explore and change this world in some way. I want to bring my uniqueness and creativity into the entertainment industry and bring a new type of flavor to it. I plan on studying psychology and massage therapy in college as back up careers. I want to someday be a role model like Tyra Banks and I hope to one day get the chance to host her show with her.

King Sami is an 18-year-old senior at King College Prep High School in Chicago. He aspires to be an engineer after completing high school. Outside of school, he enjoys playing basketball.

My name is Daria Siler. I attend King College Prep High School in Chicago. I am an honors student and I'm a junior. A year from now, I plan to go away to a small university. I want to either be an event planner, pharmacist, or an accountant. My goal throughout life is to make a difference in children's lives and become a successful role model for my niece. Education to me is the key to all success.

My name is Aaron Shannon and I am 16 years old. I attend King College Prep, where I am currently in my junior year. I enjoy playing basketball, football, and baseball. After high school, I plan on going to college to earn my B.A. degree in business administration. Then, after college, I plan on enlisting in the United States Navy.

Monique Ratcliff is a sophomore at Bronzeville Military Academy. She has been an active member in the Stand Up! Help Out! Program since Summer 2008.

Domonique Ratcliff is a sophomore at Bronzeville Military Academy. She has been an active member in the Stand Up! Help Out! Program since Summer 2008.

 My name is Desiree Tellis and I am 17 years old. I was born in Chicago, Illinois on December 18th, 1992. I am a junior at King College Prep High School. I have three sisters and no brothers. After high school I plan on pioneering, which is an activity in which I devote 80 hours of my time each month to preach to people about Jehovah (God). I also plan on attending the University of Chicago or Northwestern in order to pursue a career in business & finance, or computer technology. My goal in life is to be content and to help others to learn to do the same and also to help others to learn how they can have peaceful lives.

# REFERENCES

## Foreword

Gilbert, P. (2005). Compassion and cruelty: A biopsychoso-
cial approach. In P. Gilbert (Ed)., *Compassion: Con-
ceptualizations, research and use in psychothera-
py,* (pp. 9-74). London, Routledge.

Keyes, C. & J. E. Haidt (2003). *Flourishing: Positive psychology and the life well-lived.* Washington, D.C.

King, M. L., Jr. (1991). *A testament of hope: The essential
writings and speeches of Martin Luther King, Jr.*
San Francisco: 1st Harper Collins.

Lama, D. (2001). *An open heart: Practicing compassion in
everyday life* (Ed. by N. Vreeland). New York: Little
Brown.

Nouwen, H. J. M., D. P. McNeill, et al. (1982). *Compassion: A
reflection on the Christian life.* New York: Doubleday
Image Books.

Nussbaum, M. (2001). *Upheavals of thought: The intelligence
of emotions.* Cambridge: Cambridge University Press.

## Chapter 1

Bronfenbrenner, U. (1997). Ecological models of human development. In M. Gauvain & M. Cole (Eds.), *Readings
on the development of children* (2nd ed., pp. 37-43).
New York: Freeman

Bulanda, J. J. (2008) *Real talk: Findings from a youth-led evaluation of an after school leadership development program* (Doctoral Dissertation). Available from ProQuest Dissertations and Theses database. (UMI No. 3340153)

Crick, N. & Dodge, K. (1994). A review and reformulation of social information-processing mechanisms in children's social adjustment. *Psychological Bulletin,* 115, 74-101.

Elliot, D., Hamburg, B., & Williams, K. (1998). *Violence in American schools: New perspectives and solutions.* New York: Cambridge University Press.

Farrell, A. D. & Flannery, D. J. (2006). Youth violence prevention: Are we there yet? *Aggression and Violent Behavior,* 11, 138-150.

Graczyk, P. A. & Tolan, P. H. (2005). Implementing effective youth violence prevention programs in community settings. In R. G. Steele and M. C. Roberts (Eds.), *Handbook of mental health services for children, adolescents, and families* (pp. 215-230). New York: Kluwer Academic Publishing.

Guerra, N. G., & Bradshaw, C. P. (Eds.). (2008). Core competencies to prevent problem behaviors and promote positive youth development. *New Directions for Child and Adolescent Development,* 122.

Huesmann, L. R. (1998). The role of social information processing and cognitive schema in the acquisition and maintenance of habitual aggressive behavior. In R.G. Green & E. Donnerstein (Eds.), *Human aggression: Theories, research, and implications for social policy* (pp. 73-109). Orlando, FL: Academic Press.

Kohn, A. (1990). *The brighter side of human nature: Altruism and empathy in everyday life.* New York: Basic Books.

Loeber, R. & Stouthamer-Loeber, M. (1998). Juvenile aggression at home and at school. In D.S. Elliott, B. A. Hamburg, & K. R. Williams (Eds.), *Violence in American schools: A new perspective* (pp. 94-126). New York: Cambridge University Press.

Singer, M., Miller, D.B., Guo, S., Flannery, D., J., Freierson, T., & Slovak, K. (1999). Contributors to violent behavior among elementary and middle school children, *Pediatrics*, 104, 878-884.

Tolan, P. (2000). Youth violence and its prevention in the United States: An overview of current knowledge. *Injury Control and Safety Promotion*, 8 (1), 1-12.

U.S. Department of Health and Human Services. (2001). *Youth violence: A report of the surgeon general.* Washington, DC: United States Department of Justice.

Zeldin, S. (2004). Preventing youth violence through the promotion of community engagement and membership. *Journal of Community Psychology*, 32(5), 623-641.

## CHAPTER 2

Buzzle.com. "Domestic Violence Statistics." http://www.buzzle.com/editorials/7-24-2003-43341.asp (Accessed December 19, 2009).

Rozas, A. "2008 saw increased violence in Chicago, statistics show" http://archives.chicagotribune.com/2009/jan/17/local/chi-chicago-crime-statsjan17 (Accessed December 19, 2009)

Rozas, A. & Sandovi, C. "Weis, Huberman take on youth violence." http://www.chicagobreakingnews.com/2009/03/cps-ups-number-of-students-slain-to-27.html (Accessed December, 19, 2009).

Tolan, P. (2000). Youth violence and its prevention in the United States: An overview of current knowledge. *Injury Control and Safety Promotion*, 8 (1), 1-12.

U.S. Department of Health and Human Services. (2001).
*Youth violence: A report of the surgeon general.*
Washington, DC: United States Department of Justice.

LaVergne, TN USA
08 April 2010
178578LV00001B/203/P